The
Pondok
& Madrasah
in Patani

Monograph Series of Malay World and Civilisation

Published under the auspices of the
Institute of Malay World and Civilisation (ATMA)
Series Editor: Wan Hashim Wan Teh Ph.D.

Ismail Hamid. 1983. *The Malay Islamic Hikayat.* ISBN 967-942-011-6

Inon Shaharuddin. 1983. *Si Miskin: A Structural Study.*
ISBN 967-942-012-4

Ajid Che Kob. 1985. *Dialek Geografi Pasir Mas.* ISBN 967-942-024-8

B.A. Hussainmiya. 1990. *Orang Rejimen: The Malays of the Ceylon Rifle Regiment,* ISBN 967-942-165-1

Wan Hashim Wan Teh. 1995. *Peasants Under Peripheral Capitalism* (Second Print). ISBN 967-942-119-8

Liang Liji. 1996. *Lembaran Sejarah Gemilang: Hubungan Empayar Melaka – Dinasti Ming Abad ke-15.* ISBN 967-942-335-2

Ismail Yusoff. 1997. *Politik dan Agama di Sabah.* ISBN 967-942-381-6

Kong Yuanzhi. 2000. *Pelayaran Zheng He dan Alam Melayu.*
ISBN 967-942-508-8

Luisa J. Mallari. 2002. *From Domicile to Domain: The Formation of Malay and Tagalog Masterpiece Novels in Post-Independence Malaysia and the Philippines.* ISBN 967-942-553-3

Hasan Madmarn. 2002. *The Pondok & Madrasah in Patani* (Second Print). ISBN 967-942-403-0

The Pondok & Madrasah in Patani

HASAN MADMARN

PENERBIT UNIVERSITI KEBANGSAAN MALAYSIA
BANGI • 2002
www.penerbit.ukm.my

Cetakan Pertama / *First Printing,* 1999
Cetakan Kedua / *Second Printing,* 2002
Hak cipta / *Copyright* Universiti Kebangsaan Malaysia, 1999

Diterbitkan di Malaysia oleh / *Published in Malaysia by*
PENERBIT UNIVERSITI KEBANGSAAN MALAYSIA
43600 UKM Bangi, Selangor D.E. Malaysia
http://www.penerbit.ukm.my

Penerbit UKM adalah anggota / *is a member of the*
PERSATUAN PENERBIT BUKU MALAYSIA /
MALAYSIAN BOOK PUBLISHERS ASSOCIATION
No. Ahli / *Membership No.* 8302

Dicetak di Malaysia oleh / *Printed in Malaysia by*
MALINDO PRINTERS SDN BHD
Lot 3, Jalan Ragum, Seksyen 15/17,
46000 Shah Alam, Selangor D.E.
MALAYSIA

Perpustakaan Negara Malaysia   *Cataloguing-in-Publication Data*

Hasan Madmarn
    The pondok and madrasah in Patani / Hasan Madmarn
    1. Islamic education – Thailand – Patani
    2. Religious institutions – Thailand – Patani
    I. Judul.
    371.07709593

ISBN 967-942-403-0

Contents

List of Plates...7

Preface...9

Chapter 1   Historical Background...*11*

Chapter 2   The Pondok and its Contributions...*17*

Chapter 3   The Patani Ulama and their Roles in Islamic Education...*33*

Chapter 4   The Kitab Jawi as the Basic Foundation of Islamic Knowledge...*49*

Chapter 5   The Pondok and the Process of Change...*55*

Chapter 6   Central Government Efforts...*91*

Chapter 7   The Goverment's Initiative and Response...*102*

Chapter 8   Conclusion...123

Bibliography...129

Index...141

List of Plates

The Plates are between page - 64-65

Plate 1   The arch of Pondok Berming
Plate 2   Pondok Berming
Plate 3   The sign to the Islamic charity body in Pondok Dalo
Plate 4   This is called Pondok Dalae in the vicinity of Pondok Dalo. Pondok
           Dalae are meant for married couples only
Plate 5   Pondok Babayeh in Toyong, Patani
Plate 6   The entrance to Pondok Mak Dagae
Plate 7   Pondok Haji Mak Dagae in Naprado, Patani
Plate 8   The house of Tuan Guru Haji Mak Dagae
Plate 9   The *Balaisah* in Pondok Mango
Plate10   This is the sign of *Makam Syuhada* 'Dato Panglima Kampong Tok
           Semla Patani Darulsalam in Pondok Semla
Plate11   The Islamic Committee of Patani
Plate12   Daru'ma'arif Institute, in the Patronage by the Islamic Committee of
           Patani
Plate13   Arabic School known as Darun Sat School in Saiburu, Patani
Plate14   College of Islamic Studies, Prince of Songkla University, Patani
Plate15   Saudara Press, serve as both the bookstore and printing house
Plate16   Taman Pustaka Press, produces the works of the present generation
           of religious teachers of Patani
Plate17   Haris Trading was opened in 1939, distributing religious books to
           Pondok in various parts of Patani
Plate18   Mohammad Nahdi Bookstore, one of the Muslim bookstore in
           downtown area of Patani
Plate19   Masjid Jamek Patani
Plate20   Masjid Cabang Tiga Patani
Plate21   Kitab Minhaj al-Abidin ila Jannat Rabb al-Alamin
Plate22   Kitab Munyat al-Musalli by Shaykh Dawud bin Abdullah al-Fatani
Plate23   Kitab Faridat al-Faraid fi Ilm al-Aqaaid by Shaykh Ahmad bin
           Muhammad Zayn bin Mustafa al-Fatani
Plate24   Kitab Bahjat al-Mubtadin Wa-Farhat al-Mujtadin discusses ilm usul
           al-din and fiqh relating to ritual obligation
Plate25   Kitab Kashf al-Litham an Asilat al-Anam
Plate 26   Kitab Idah al-Bab Li-Murid al-Nikah bi-al-Sawab

Preface

The objective of this book is to draw the attention of readers to the important function of the Patani ulama whose fame goes back to the time when Patani was the cradle of Islam. It is written with the intention to bring Patani and her people to the international academic arena, so that the vital role of Patani in various aspects could be easily understood by the world outside. This is because the eminent role of the Patani ulama has never been erased from the memory of the Muslim world especially the Islamic scholars.

The traditional Islamic institutions were disturbed when the new education policy incorporated Thai education into the pondok institution. Since before the 1950's, the Thai government policy towards education became stronger and more aware of the need of a national awareness-oriented education. The vital function of the traditional Islamic institution (the pondok) was seen by the authorities as non-beneficial to the society. However, the Muslim community in Thailand believes that the institution will help the people become good citizens and be more loyal to the country.

Therefore, to maintain their traditional Islamic heritage, they had to adjust from being static to being more dynamic. This led them to play a more prominent role discussing with the authorities on how to have a model society. Consequently, the new generation were encouraged to study in various fields both in local institution and abroad. However, they are first inculcated with the virtue of self-reliance and a sense of responsibility.

Though Patani today is only a small town in southern Thai, her past reputation and greatness in academic performance still stay with the scholars of the Patani ulama and their classical works on Kitab Jawi, like those of Shaykh Daud al-Fatani, Shaykh Ahmad bin Muhammad Zayn al-Fatani and other contemporaries in the Malay-speaking world like Tok Kenali, Nik Mahmud bin Nik Ismail, and Shaykh Mahmud Sa'id, the mufti of Negeri Sembilan.

Finally, thousands of thanks should be given to the editorial staff of Penerbit Universiti Kebangsaan Malaysia who have spent a lot of their time to present this book in good shape. One should not forget those who help to get this book published such as Tan Sri Professor Dr. Awang Had Salleh and Datuk Professor Dr. Wan Hashim Wan Teh. May Allah reward their good intention.

Hasan Madmarn
College of Islamic Studies
Prince of Songkla University
Patani, Thailand

CHAPTER 1
Historical Background

The history of Patani, once referred to as a Malay kingdom, dates back as far as the early thirteenth century, when the Sukothai kings of Siam (later called Thailand) claimed the Muslim Sultanates as vassals (Suhrake & Noble 1977). For centuries, Patani teetered between independence and conquest by Siam. The name of Patani is found in several sixteenth century records (Froser 1960). They indicate that it was a prosperous state that served as an international entrepot on the east coast of the Malay peninsula.

In 1612, the first British ship to visit Patani, the *Globe*, anchored off the coast, bringing among its merchant-passengers Peter Floris who recorded the course of the voyage and later composed a short history. The year of the arrival of the *Globe* at the Patani entrepot must be determined from the account given in the *Voyage of Floris to the East Indies*. In this record, we find that *Floris* left Masulipatam (a seaport in India), sailing for Bantam in Jawa on 1st of February, 1612. He reached Bantam, the most important seaport in Jawa and the second visit, on the 26th of April of the same year.

After a short stay, he discovered that the commercial conditions prevailing in Bantam were at that time unfavorable for trade, sailed for Patani (Floris 1934). Virginia Thompson wrote that "after the Portuguese had captured Melaka in 1511, they sent two embassies to Ayuthia to establish trade relations in Patani." When Melaka fell into the hand of the Dutch in 1641, they conducted their trade and began to establish a relationship with the Kingdom of Patani (Thompson 1941).

Patani, situated on the east coast of southern Thailand, was for centuries the seat of a Malay Kingdom (Jones 1979). Patani, in those ancient and glorious days, was controlled by the Malay Sultanate. Vestiges of its dynasty and importance remain until today, for the Malay-Muslim community of Patani speak the Malay language in their daily lives and are quite different from their fellow Thai citizens in terms of customs, religion and thought. It is most likely that these features will serve as everlasting reminders of its past glory (Mathesan & Hooker 1988). Furthermore, if one wonders how and why the Malay-Muslims of Patani remain so distinct from their fellow Thai citizens, recall that the history of the Malay city-state has been recorded and studied, generation upon generation.

Present-day Patani is one of the four southernmost provinces of Thailand which comprise, Yala, Narathiwat and Satun. Most of the Malays of Thailand live within these four provinces. Songkla province is also officially included among the southern border provinces. It lies between Satun in the west and Yala and Patani provinces to the southeast and east respectively. It has a substantial Malay minority, a large part of which is found in the city of Songkla and in the major districts like Hat Yai, Sadao, Rattaphum, Chana, Nathawee, Tepha and Sabayoi.

From Songkla province or Hat Yai district, the journey by car to Patani following the newly-constructed highway along the seashore takes about one hour and a half. On the way to Patani, not far from Songkla province, there is a famous district (Amphôe in Thai) called Chana which was a center of traditional Islamic teaching.

Patani, in the early nineteenth century, became the center of traditional Islamic education to which the Muslims get their early education in Islam before transferring them to Middle Eastern institutions, especially to study under the tutelage of the teachers at the Holy Mosque in Mecca. Patani had preserved a unique religious and cultural character and institutions which could not be found elsewhere in the region. Among these were well-known *pondok* and their respective *tok guru*. Through them, Patani was able to attract students from all over the area. Patani in fact earned a title as "an early center of Islam," and as the "cradle of Islam in Southeast Asia" (Pitsuwan 1982) as well. The well-known pondok of Patani in those days, some of which still exist, included Pondok Dalo, whose teacher was Haji Abd. al-Rahman, known as Tok Dalo; Pondok Semla, whose teacher was Haji Ismail, known as Tok Semla; Pondok Bermin, whose teacher was Haji Ahmad bin Idris, known as Tok Bermin; Pondok Mango, whose teacher was Haji Hasan, known as Tok Mango; and many others not recorded, scattered around Patani province. These are not exact record as to when the first pondok of Patani was founded, nor of the dates of establishment of the schools and teachers mentioned here in. However, the pondok named were among the most well-known traditional institution in those days. Haji Abd al-Latif bin Haji Wan Muhammad Nur, the current Mudîr or Director of Mahad al-Ulum, Jerang Batu, Patani, can still recall other well known pondok that no longer exist, such as Pondok Duku, Pondok Bego (Bero), Pondok Telukmanok, Pondok Bendang Daya, Pondok Bendang Guchil and Pondok Chuwuk.

The graduates of these pondok were numerous. Some of them became religious teachers themselves and role models in the Muslim community, providing Islamic education for the Muslim people as their ancestors used to do.

The Coming of Islam into Patani

There is no firmly-established date for the coming of Islam into Patani, but one source states that Patani adopted Islam before Melaka and traditionally Patani was known as the first abode of peace (Mills 1930). D.G.E. Hall gives a possible date for the arrival of Islam in Terengganu, an east-coast state of Malaysia and a neighbour of Patani, by saying "So far as the Peninsula is concerned, the earliest Islamic document is a stone inscription at Terengganu with its date defaced. It is somewhere between 1303 and 1387." (Hall 1955). However, Hall asserts that Patani was converted from Melaka during the latter half of the fifteenth century. Kelantan received Islam as a dependency of Patani. Russell Jones on the other hand, indicates that the date of Patani's conversion to Islam is very uncertain, being possibly more towards the end of the fifteenth century. Patani's acceptance of Islam, he says, is of particular significance in that it marks the limit of the spread of Islam in the Malay Peninsula (Jones 1979).

Patani, as mentioned earlier, was rule by the Malay Raja (kings) who in those days were not Muslims. Therefore "the commoners in Patani continued to follow the religion introduced (earlier) by the Hindu; the Buddhist religion of the Mahayana sect." (Syukri 1985). In fact, this region was first influenced by Hinduism, then Buddhism and finally Islam took over and helds way. It is clear that Islam introduced a new dimension to the region's history. Prior to Islam, Hinduism and Buddhism had served as the basis for the region's cultures and civilizations. According to Ibrahim Syukri,

On the Island of Sumatra there existed a country named Pasai whose residents had embraced the Islamic religion, but surrounding their country there were still many people of the Hindu religion. Therefore, the country of Pasai was frequently attacked by Hindus causing the Muslims to endure a life of hardship. Some of them left for other countries to save themselves. Among them were those who fled in the direction of Patani, so that Patani began to receive Muslims arriving from Pasai. They built a village there, all the residents of which were people from Pasai and the village was named Kampung Pasai as it is today.

(Syukri 1985)

From Ibrahim Syukri's account we can infer that among the people who arrived in Patani there must have been some learned and well-equipped men who knew, at least, about the basic principle of Islam. Because of the Pasai Muslim people, Islam gained a vital foothold, spreading later across fertile soils of Patani. Pasai was the seaport that provided what was possibly the earliest growing point for Islam in Sumatra (Harrison 1954). This is strongly confirmed by A.H. Johns when he says, "Much has been written on the origins of Islamization in Southeast Asia, usually beginning with Pasai and other port towns along the northeast coast of Sumatra (Johns 1976).

According to A. Teeuw and D.K. Wyatt, the Islamization of Patani began when King Phaya Tu Nakpa, who had reigned over Patani for several years, embraced Islam. This occurred when King Phaya Tu Nakpa fell ill with a skin disease which caused his skin to crack. None of those astrologers and doctors who were asked could prescribe therapy which could heal such a skin disease. His illness grew even more serious. Upon hearing the reports made by the heralds who were beating the gong as told in *The Story of Patani,* Shaykh Said who was sitting among others at the religious center of Kampung Pasai, Patani determined to undertake to cure the king's illness on condition he would then be willing to become a Muslim. The King, who had in desperation promised his daughter in marriage to whomsoever could cure his illness was at last taken under the care of Shaykh Said. Shaykh Said, who had originally come from Pasai, Aceh, in Indonesia, did not seem to be interested in the king's offer. Rather, if the disease were cured and the king recovered, Shaykh Said asked that the king would embrace Islam. Fortunately, the medical treatment was effective, the disease was cured and the king was restored to health. Thereafter, the promise made was kept. In front of his ministers, officers and subjects, Shaykh Said taught King Phaya Tuk Nakpa the Kalimah *Shahâdah*, the Statement of Belief, which runs, "I profess that there is no god but Allah and I profess that Muhammad is Allah's messenger," After the king had pronounced the Statement of Belief, Shaykh Said taught it to all his ministers, officers and such subjects as were present as well. The king was immediately renamed Sultan Ismail Shah Zillullah fî al-Alam.

When the old king passed away, his eldest son, Sultan Mudhaffar Syah (Muzaffar Shah) succeeded to the throne. At that time, the sultan and his younger brother Sultan Manzur Syah (Mansur Shah) had expressed a need to know more about Islam. Thus it was that they asked Shaykh Safyuddin for his wisdom. Shaykh Safyuddin, a learned man also from Pasai, Aceh, Indonesia, took this opportunity to inform the king that a Muslim community needs to have a place to perform the Islamic rituals and that a mosque should be built for this purpose. Upon hearing that, the Sultan ordered the prime minister to have a mosque built as it had been proposed by the Shaykh. Eventually, the Shaykh was appointed to teach Islamic law in the palace and was given the elevated title of Datuk Sri Raja Faqih. Thus did the royal court of Patani became the center for the spreading of Islam in the region (Teeuw & Wyatt 1970).

The Patani People, their Customs and their Language

The Muslim people of Patani preserve characteristics and an identity different from their fellow Thais in other parts of the country. These distinguishing characteristics also apply to those living in the other three Malay-speaking areas, that is, Yala, Narathiwat and Satun and also those who live in the districts of Songkla such as Chana, Nathawee, Tepha and Sabayoi. In all these area, the people speak Malay, though with dialects and accents which are slightly different from each other. On the other hand, both the accent and dialect of Satun are similar to those of Perlis and Kedah, the two northtern states of Malaysia, while the dialect and accent of those who live in Patani, Yala and Narathiwat are much more akin to those spoken in Kelantan. Among the people themselves, accent and the dialect are the best indicators of their geographical origins. Through conversation, one can easily tell from which area another speaker comes.

The daily dress of the people in these regions, both men and women, is typically different from that worn in other parts of the country. The most typical features of dress among the Patani people and other Malay-speaking group resemble closely those of Kelantan as described by Winzeler:

The pious man is also marked by his dress and his moral behaviour. The most ubiquitous item of dress which serves to differentiate those who occupy some special religious status from those who do not is the white skull cap (kupiah). This is the mark of the religious student and the returned Haji, but the wearing of it, rather than the dark felt *songkok* or, in the case of many villagers, the colored head scarf, serves to signify religious status in general. In the case of at least the more important religious figures the *kupiah* is supplemented by other items, most importantly the white head scarf (serban) which is wrapped into a turban or draped about the neck.
(Winzeler 1974)

The people in the Patani area tend to speak Malay (*kecek nayu*: Malay vernacular) in their ordinary conversation and in their daily round of activities. Most of them can communicate in the Thai language. However, they prefer speaking the Malay language because it is their mother tongue. They teach their young children to imitate them, speaking not in Thai, but in Malay. These young children usually start to pick up the Thai language as soon as they are sent to preschools or, if fortunate enough to have a bilingual parent, they may learn it from their mothers. Watching television is another means for them to learn to speak Thai.

For the typical Malay Muslim of the area, the Malay language means to them more than one can imagine. Malay, or Melayu for them, is understood both as the mother tongue and the sign of a person who embraces Islam. In other words, speaking Melayu is synonymous with being a Muslim. The Malay language has strong connection with Islam and religious heritage and it is strongly related to Islamic literature, especially when referring to those religious books written in Jawi. This issue will be addressed in the following chapter. A Muslim, knowing how to speak Melayu is, in the eyes of Patani Muslims, usually considered to be a good person. In a sense, a person able to speak Malay may be looked upon as having preserved a Muslim identity. However, not all those who speak Malay can then be considered to be members of Muslim society. This is a very complicated issue.

The Community and its Economic Resources

As a consequence of the fact that most Malay-Muslim communities in the four southern provinces are located in rural areas, their source of income is primarily agricultural. They are farmers, working in padi-fields, or market gardeners, working on their small pieces of land, growing coconuts, oil palms and fruit as well as tapping rubber trees. Those who live in the coastal areas are engaged mostly in small-scale fishing activities. Because the income of Malay-Muslim communities is derived from work affected by seasonal change, they are often involved in more than one means of making a living. Some, for example, work in padi-fields during the day and go fishing in coastal waters when night falls (Madmarn 1988).

CHAPTER 2

The Pondok and its Contributions

Traditional Islamic Education in Chana District, Songkla

Between the 1930's and the 1950's Chana, a town in Songkla Province became very popular with the Muslim communities, both Malay and Thai-speaking, as a place where in one could obtain a traditional Islamic education. This town, with its well-known pondok and its learned tok guru, used to attract young Muslims, mostly from Nakorn Si Thammaraj, Trang, Krabi, Pangnga, Surat Thani, Phuket, Patthalung, Chaiya and Songkla and also from the four southern provinces.

In the year 1955, there were several pondok scattered around the Chana district providing a basic Islamic education but only four major prestigious and highly regarded pondok in the town of Chana. These pondok were named after their tok guru and were:

1. Pondok Tok Guru Haji Nor; known as Ayah Nor (Muhammad Nur).
2. Pondok Tok Guru Haji Leh (Haji Salih).
3. Pondok Tok Guru Haji Somad (Haji Abd al-Samad).
4. Pondok Tok Guru Ghani known as Pondok Padang Langa.

The Pondok Tok Guru Haji Nor was located in the northern part of the town, the Pondok Tok Guru Haji Leh and the Pondok Tok Guru Haji Somad were located east and west of the Chana railway station respectively and the Pondok Tok Guru Ghani was located a half-hour walk out of town to the south in a place known as Padang Langa. The first three of those pondok were renowned because their tok guru were well-versed in classical Islamic works translated into Jawi and in the Kitab Jawi; treatises written mostly by the ulama of Patani and men such as Shaykh Dawud al-Fatani, and Shaykh Ahmad al-Fatani. Besides their reputation for having a broad knowledge of Islamic disciplines and individual specialties in certain areas, they were also known as the Tok Guru Kaum Tua or orthodox religious teachers, literally, the 'old group'. These men, among other things, restricted themselves to the settled opinions on correct Islamic conduct as found in the ulama of the Shafii school of law and Islamic precepts taken solely from the accepted handbooks of the Shafii school of law. These Tok Guru Kaum Tua usually looked at those intellects who tried to extract Islamic precepts directly from the Quran and Hadith as the Kaum Muda or modern group, literally the 'young group'. In short, as William Roff says, "to be Kaum Muda came to mean espousal of modernism in any form; to be Kaum Tua was to be in favour of all that was traditional, unchanging and secure (Roff in Ibrahim et al. 1985).

It is worth mentioning here that the three main issues that brought out conflict among these tok guru's were:

1. The *Talqîn al-mayyit* (traditional reading of instructions to the dead over the grave immediately after he/she was buried).
2. *Usallî* (literally, "I pray," pronounced by some Muslims in Southeast Asia at the very beginning of each prayer before saying "Allahu Akhbar") (Nik Abdul Aziz 1977).
3. The *al-Muhallil*. The *muhallil* is a man who marries a thrice-divorce woman with the intention of making her subsequent remarriage with the first husband legal. This subterfuge (*hîlah*) came into existence because Islamic law did not allow the remarriage of a man to a woman already divorced three times by him unless there was an intervening marriage and divorce to another man (Quran II. 229-230). In this case, the ex-husband would make a secret agreement with someone, usually and old blind man thought physically incapable of having sexual relations with the ex-wife, to get married to her on the condition that the man (*muhallil*, literally, 'who makes lawful') must divorce the woman as soon as possible after the marriage ceremony had been performed. Through the secret agreement, the ex-husband, of course, must give the *muhallil* (the second supposed husband) a certain amount of money for playing this role. The custom of using a *muhallil* in such cases was and still is severely condemned by the Kaum Muda. This man is known throughout the Malay-Muslim community as a *Cina Buta* ('a blind Chinese man') or Chîn Ta Bód in Thai. The Tok Guru Kaum Muda look at such practices as diseases endemic in society that should be totally abolished and eradicated. Tok Guru Ghani, originally from Kelantan, of Pondok Padang Langa, stood against these practices and was ready to debate on the issues whenever it was necessary. He taught his students to understand the meaning of the Quran and the Hadith correctly. The first two issues mentioned above deal with the positive rules for the application of Islamic law, the *furû'*, rather than the theory or root of Islamic law, the *usûl*. Thus, the arguments between the Kaum Tua and the Kaum Muda of the Malay-speaking community were and are purely religious, having nothing to do with the administrative structure of the Muslim community as perceived by the Muslims in Bangkok, the capital of Thailand. They are also issues hotly debated by Muslim communities in Indonesia (Noer 1973).

Dr. Raymond Scupin explains that there are two groups, known in the Thai-speaking community as *Khana Mai* (new group) and *Khana Kau* (old group). These two groups are those referred to among the Malay-speaking people of southern Thailand as the Kaum Muda dan Kaum Tua previously described. The *Khana Mai* group, who is also known as the reformists, besides involving themselves in religious issues call for a return to deriving rules for conduct directly from the primary sources, the Quran and Hadith and for a reconsideration of the structures of Muslim society in Thailand. As Raymond Scupin says:

The *khana mai* viewed themselves as representing the true faith of Islam in the midst of what they perceived as the backwardness of Muslim thought in Thailand. But in addition, Islamic reformism was seen as a vehicle for instituting socioeconomic and political changes for the Muslims of Thailand. Thai Islamic reformist ideology emphasized egalitarian principles and contained within it a critique of any kind of absolute authority including that of the Chularajmontri (a Shaykh al-Islam in Thailand). The *khana mai* Muslims sought to transform the nature of Thai polity in order to further the social and political interests of their Muslim brethren.

(Scupin in Asian Survey vol 20. 1980)

If we compare the *Khana Mai* of Muslim in Bangkok and the Kaum Muda of Malay-Muslims in southern Thailand, then it is clear that the latter have solely emphasized a series of religious issues, though these involve societal matters such as the rules on marriage and divorce. The *Khana Mai,* however, have been concerned with sociopolitical issues entailed by the position of the Muslim community as a minority religious group in a largely Buddhist country. Among these issues are the appointment and status of the Shaykh al-Islam, a religious advisor to the Thai Government on all matters concerning the promotion of Islam and matters concerning Provincial Council for Muslims, through which each Provincial is authorized by law to appoint a council for each mosque within the boundaries of the province (Thailand [Yearbook] 1964: 513).

Tok Guru Ghani has since been labeled as the major protagonist of the Kaum Muda group as a result of trying to correct certain long-standing aberrations in religious practice that he labeled as innovation (*bid'ah*), though they were common in Malay-Muslim society.

Tok Guru Ghani, whose real name was Abdul Ghani Fikri, was a native of Kelantan, Malaysia. He was a young local scholar when he was invited to teach at Padang Langa by Tok Guru Abd al-Samad, some years before 1955. In Padang Langa, Tok Guru Ghani received a warm welcome from the Muslim communities of Kampung Kok Ked, Kampung Padang Langa, Kampung Padang and Kampung Namkim in Chana district. He had three younger brothers, Che' Samae, Che' Omar and Che' Mat Ali. His mother, whom the students call *Mak Su,* was a humble, pious woman and the family was a very ordinary one without any special social status. His wife, a native of Kelantan, whom we call *Mak Cik*, is now living next to my brother's house in Gombak, Selangor, Malaysia.

Before Tok Guru Abdul Ghani Fikri passed away on November 28, 1982, I was fortunate to meet him for the last time in Kampung Nakhoda at Batu Caves, Selangor, Malaysia. His left side was paralysed and, with feelings of melancholy, I embraced him as a sign of farewell, expecting never to see him again. The late Tok Guru Ghani (b. 1929, d. 11/28/1982), the product of a pondok in Terengganu, and a *murid* (student) of Pondok Ahmadiyah Bunut Payong and Masjid Besar al-Muhammadi, Kota Bharu, Kelantan, Malaysia, preserved a deep knowledge of Islam and was fluent in Arabic. At the Masjid Besar al-Muhammadi, Tok Guru Ghani studied under Datuk Haji Muhammad Noor Bin Haji Ibrahim known as Shaykh Nor, the late *Mufti* of Kelantan (b. 8/20/1905, d. 2/13/1987).

As far as I remember, all the books he taught were Arabic books on subjects ranging from Tradition (Hadith), Quranic commentary (tafsir), Islamic jurisprudence (*fiqh*), grammar and morphology (nahw and sarf) and rhetoric (balaghah). I will mention some of those that I used to read under him, though more often under his assistants. His fame as a young tok guru, well-versed in Arabic and as a man with an excellent academic training, attracted the students from every corner of the southern Muslim communities in the period of peak popularity of the Pondok Padang Langa in the years before 1955.

In 1955, the first year of my studies at this pondok, I witnessed the arrival of perhaps hundreds of newcomers between the age of about fifteen and twenty-five. The popularity of this pondok may be attributed to some other factors in addition to the knowledgeable characteristic of Tok Guru Ghani himself. Two assets of the school were his two helpers, whom the students called Tok Guru Rashid and Tok Guru Khalid. Both of them were graduates of the Pondok Penanti, Bukit Mertajam, Malaysia. Tok Guru Abd al-Rashid bin Abd al-Mannan, a native of Negeri Sembilan, Malaysia, was responsible for books in Arabic as was his learned senior, Tok Guru Ghani. Tok Guru Khalid, on the other hand, was responsible for the books in the Malay language, the Kitab Jawi.

Another factor that made the Pondok Padang Langa famous was its classes that geared towards the system of modern madrasah, as may be found in Arab countries. This type of class was rarely found in the traditional system of the pondok in those days. In 1955, the Pondok Padang Langa had already been given the new name 'Madrasah al-Falâh al-Balâgh al-Mubîn'. It is now officially known as Rongrian Rongroch Vittaya in Thai. The main aim of the classes, as they were provided in those days, was to train the beginners to read and write Arabic as well as Jawi. The classes usually took place in the morning and were divided according to the capability of the students, yet the traditional systems of learning were strongly emphasized.

This pondok now run by al-Ustaz Haji Ibrahim bin Aqil, a graduate of Pondok Pokok Senor, Kepala Batas, Malaysia. Through these scholars and teaching innovations, the Pondok Padang Langa became a prominent center of Islamic learning and remain so until today.

It is important to differentiate between the learning system of the pondok and that of the madrasah in Thailand. The system of the former is medieval, group-learning system known as *halaqah* and characterised by a circle of students assembled around a teacher. Neither graded classes nor blackboards were provided. All the students, regardless of their ages and their backgrounds, brought their books to read in front of their tok guru in a big open hall, traditionally known as a *balaisah,* three times a day. They learned by jotting down the explanations and the commentaries that they heard from their teachers. The beginners learned together with the seniors and juniors. No classification separated them according to their background. Most of the students learned by rote. There is no examination nor assessment process contained within this system, nor even a limit of time for studying. A student can continue to study to the highest level of competency and may stay up to ten years or more if needed.

The madrasah system, in contrast, is like the typical system of its kind found in Muslim countries. The madrasah system in Thailand paves the way for its students to further their education at higher levels in those other countries in instructional mediums other than their mother tongue.

Some of the books that were used as texts at this pondok are as follows:
1. *al-Muwatta'*, the early legal work of Imam Malik ibn Anas al-Asbahi (d. 795).
2. *Sahih al-Bukhari* of Abu Abd Allah ibn Ismail ibn Ibrahim ibn Bardizbah al-Jufi al-Bukhari (d.256 A.H).
3. *Bulûgh al-Murâm min Adillat al-Ahkâm* (*fiqh*) by al-Hafiz Ahmad ibn Ali ibn Hajar al-Asqalani (773-852 A.H.).
4. *Tafsîr al-Jalâlayn.* The Qur'an commentary by Jalal al-Din Muhammad ibn Ahmad al-Mahalli (1389-1459) and Jalal al-Din Abd al-Rahman ibn Abi Bakr al-Suyuti (1445-1505).
5. *Kitâb al-Iqnâ 'fi hall alfâz Abî Shujâ`* (*fiqh*) by Muhammad al-Shirbini al-Khatib. (d. 1570).
6. *Kitâb Shadhâ al-'Uzaf fî Fann al-Sarf* (morphology) by Shaykh Ahmad al-Hamlawi.
7. *Matn al-Binâ' wa-al-Asâs* (morphology) by Allamat Mulla Abd Allah al-Danaqzi.
8. *Matn al-Ajurrûmîyah* (grammar) by Abu Abd Allah Muhammad ibn Dawud al-Sinhaji known as Ibn Ajurrûm (1273 or 4-1323).
9. *Tashwîq al-Khullân 'alâ Sharh al-Ajurrûmîyah* (grammar) by Sayyid Ahmad Zayni Dahlan (1816 or 7-1886).

10. *Kitâb Jawâhir al-Maknûn* (rhetoric) by al-Shaykh Makhlûf al-Minyâwî.
11. *al-Alfîyah li-Ibn Mâlik* (grammar) by Jamal al-Din Muhammad ibn Abd Allah ibn Malik (1274).
12. *Kitâb Sharh Ibn 'Aqîl 'alâ al-Alfîyah* (grammar) by Jamal al-Din Muhammad ibn Abd Allah ibn Malik (1274).
13. *al-Iqnâ' fi Hall Alfâz Abî Shujâ'* by Shaykh Muhammad Shirbini (d. 1570).

The book mentioned above were used as the major text books in the Pondok Padang Langa and they were, in those days, available in the 'Kedai Jual Kitab Arab dan Jawi', the Malay bookstore of Haji Che' Omar Ali Ishaq (d. April 2, 1989) in downtown Chana. I believe these kitab were also used as texts and taught in the other pondok in Chana and Patani as well.

The Patani Ulama and their Works

To give an idea of the role and scholarly contribution of the ulama of Patani, four much-acclaimed writers and some of their works as an indication of how far and for how long the influence of the Arabic and Islamic literature of Patani has penetrated into the Muslim populace will be cited, both inside and outside Patani. These writers are Shaykh Dawud, Shaykh Ahmad, Shaykh Zayn al-Abidin bin Muhammad al-Fatani, and Shaykh Muhammad bin Ismail Dawud.

Shaykh Dawud and Shaykh Ahmad are popular to the degree that their names are closely related to Greater Patani, once a great center of Islamic intellectual learning several decades ago. By the same token, Patani, even today, when mentioned to Muslim intellectuals, reminds them of its past glory as an intellectual center. One reason may be that the books of Shaykh Dawud and the other three nineteenth-century Patani scholars are used outside Patani and are also published in several other places, among them Malaysia, Singapore, Indonesia and even in Egypt. Oddly, they are not published in Patani itself (Matheson & Hooker 1988).

Patani scholars of the nineteenth century and their works are well-known not only to the Muslim community in Thailand, but also to those in Malaysia, Indonesia and even in Cambodia. Some of their works have been copied and reprinted from the very early days of the nineteenth century down to the present. At this time many local Patani Muslim scholars of Kitab Jawi are still actively producing Islamic treatises to feed the intellectual needs of the Muslim community. They are mostly of the generation born in the 1920's.

Among the scholars named above, the first two, Shaykh Ahmad bin Muhammad Zayn bin Mustafa bin Muhammad al-Fatani and Shaykh Dawud bin Abd Allah bin Idris al-Fatani, are usually mentioned side by side, though Shaykh Dawud is often ranked a little higher. However, Shaykh Ahmad, in terms of his educational philosophical influence upon the ulama of Kota Bharu, Kelantan, Malaysia, is ranked in line with Shah Waliyullah al-Dahlawi and Maulana Abd Allah al-Sindi (Haji Nik Hassan 1977). His brief biography tells us that he was born in 1856 in Kampung Jambu, Jaring, Patani; and died in 1906. He was a descendant of a Hadramawt preacher who came to preach Islam in Patani. He received a thorough Islamic education in Mecca. There, he learned medicine under an Indian physician, Shaykh Abd al-Rahim al-Kabuli and traveled to study at Jerusalem. He finally went to study at al-Azhar University. He again returned to Masjid al-Haram, Mecca, devoting his life to teaching until he became a well-known scholar. It is related that, in the early twentieth century, the ulama of Kelantan, such as To' Kenali, Haji Wan Musa bin Haji Abd al-Samad, Haji Ibrahim and Haji Nik Mahmud bin Haji Nik Ismail studied under him (Haji Nik Hassan 1977). The following are some of the works of the four great ulama of Patani.

Shaykh Dawud al-Fatani and His Major Works
Kitâb Furû` al-Masâ'il

The book was largely translated by Shaykh Dawud al-Fatani from the *fatâwá* of Shaykh Muhammad al-Ramli and the *Kashf al-Lithâm 'an As'ilat al-Anâm* of Husayn ibn Muhammad al-Mahalli on *fiqh*. He compiled it in 1838. The first page of the first volume of this book was composed in Malay but written in Jawi script; after praising Allah and witnessing that there is no god save Allah and that Muhammad, peace be upon him, is His Messenger, Shaykh Dawud expresses his conception of the task he has undertaken by writing his introduction in Arabic saying:

In the year 1254 of the Hijrah (1838 A.D.), may the best of blessings and most peace be upon him (the Prophet), my heart was moved and my thought inclined to take up for you questions like pearls and jewels, and answers like pearls arranged on a string of explanations, and some precious branches of Islamic Law, full of satisfying benefits, from the great two books *Fatâwâ Shams al-Millah wa-al-Dîn* (The Legal Opinions of the Sun of the Religious Community and of Religion) of the strong pillar of jurists and explorers of truth, al-Shaykh Muhammad al-Ramli, and the Kitab *Kashf al-Lithâm `an As'ilat al-Anâm* (The Lifter of the Veil from the Questions of All Beings) by the later, more recent great scholar and researcher for truth, Husayn ibn Muhammad al-Mahalli, may God have a mercy upon both of them. I took from both books the religious problems to which the answers are needed by both the educated and the common believers. I named it *Furû' al-Masâ'il wa-Usûl al-Wasâ'il* (The Branches of Questions and the Roots of Means).

I asked God that He may make it beneficial for me and the Muslims and a treasure for the Day of Judgement.

(Shaykh Dawud al-Fatani)

   Printed on the margin of this book is the *Kashf al-Ghummah* (Lifter of the Cloud), a treatise by the author, explaining the situation of the deceased and the conditions of Resurrection Day. A draft of the *Furû' al-Masâ'il* was completed in Mecca, 1257 A.H. (1840/1 A.D.). It was revised by Uthman Salih al-Azhari, and printed by Dâr Ihyâ' al-Kutub al-'Arabîyah, Cairo, Egypt. This edition was reprinted by Dar al-Ma'arif, Penang, Malaysia.

Kitâb Bughyat al-Ṭullâb li-Murîd Ma'rifat al-Aḥkâm bi-al-Ṣawâb

This two-volume work focuses on religious observances (ibadat), based on commentaries on Nawawi's *Minhaj al-Talibin*, among them the *Tuḥfah* of Ibn Ḥajar al-Haitamî, the Nihayah of Ramli and the *Fatḥ al-Wahhâb* of Zakariya al-Ansari (Matheson & Hooker 1988). In the margins of this book, the Kitab *Nahj al-Râghibîn wa-Subul al-Muttaqîn* by the author is inserted. It is important to learn how Shaykh Dawud started dealing with the latter book, as he wrote, in Arabic.

It was the year 1226 of the Hijrah of the Prophet (1810/11 A.D.), peace be upon him, when some of my friends who frequented my company repeatedly asked me to translated into the Jawi tongue those things which are necessary from the rules of sales including the precepts of transactions ... from the books relied on such as *al-Minhâj, al-Tuḥfah, al-Nihâyah, al-Wahhâj, al-Manhaj, Fatḥ al-Wahhâb, al-Iqnâ'* and others ... according to the *madhhab* of the Imâm of Imâms and the Sultan of the Community, Muhammad ibn Idris al-Shafii al-Qurash, who fills the layers of the earth with knowledge ... The poor, ephemeral Dawud bin Idris al-Fatani takes as his guide what the Prophet says, "The person who directs someone to the doing of good is like the one who does it." I nevertheless acknowledge my shortcoming and limited knowledge, and cling to Allah that He may guide me into the right path ... I named this book *Well-Trodden Path of the Eager and the Ways of the Sure* with a hope it will be counted to our credit on the Promised Day and that He will inspire us with that which is correct.

(Shaykh Dawud al-Fatani)

Kitâb Minhâj al-'Abidîn ilâ Jannat Rabb al-'Alamîn

This 148 page book, which is translated from Kitab *Minhâj al-'Abidîn* of The Proof of Islam, Imam al-Ghazali of Tus, discusses Sufism. The writing and translating were completed in Mecca in 1240 A.H. (1824/5 A.D.). It was revised by al-Hajj Ilyas Ya'qub al-Azhari; and published at Dâr Ihyâ' al-

Kutub al-Arabiyah, Cairo, Egypt. This edition has been reprinted by Dar al-Ma'arif, Penang, Malaysia.

Kitâb al-Durr al-Thamîn

This is another major book of Shaykh Dawud that is quite familiar to the Muslims of Patani, especially to those students from the traditional institutions. This 103 page book, which explains the Creed *(i'tiqâd)*, was completed in Mecca in 1232 A.H. (1816/7 A.D.). It was later revised by Shaykh Ishaq ibn Ibrahim Minangkabaw and Zayn al-Abidin ibn Ibrahim al-Azhari. The book was first published in Mecca and then in Cairo by Dâr Ihyâ' al-Kutub al-'Arabîyah. It was reprinted by Dar al-Maarif, Penang, Malaysia.

Shaykh Dawud, after lauding Allah and offering prayer for the Prophet whose mission was to bring clear signs to mankind, writes in Arabic in the beginning of this book:

It was the year 1232 A.H. (1816/7 A.D.), peace be upon him when my lukewarm heart and my limited mind were moved towards compiling the words (works) of the explorers of truth (muhaqqiqîn) dealing with the sources of religious doctrine and the creed of the people who believe in God's Unity. I mention the pearls and threw away the shells, encouraging the seekers of knowledge. I have rendered them into the Jawi tongue for those who don't understand Arabic, though I am not worthy of that. But, I totally depend upon Allah, the Beneficent, the Coverer (of our errors) that He might guide me to the right path by the grace of our master, the chosen Prophet... I named this book *al-Durr al-Thamîn fî `Aqâ'id al-Mu'minîn* (The Valuable Pearl Concerning the Creeds of the Faithful). To achieve success, through Allah upon whom I have relied and to Him I turn repentantly.

(Shaykh Dawud al-Fatani 1320)

Kitâb Munyat al-Musallî

This book explains how to perform ritual prayer (solah) based on the Quran and Hadith of the Prophet, as well as the dicta of the ulama. Shaykh Dawud wrote this book mainly to teach his Malay Muslim people the proper words and gestures of prayer, beginning with raising two hands up to the shoulders while saying, *Allâhu akhbar* an action known as *takbirat al-ihram* and ending with the sitting for the last part of prayer, called *tahiyah* and *salam*. It is a very useful work for any Malay Muslim who reads Jawi and knows how to read the Quran. At the end of this book, a small but valuable treatise *al-Bahjah al-Mardîyah* (The Joy which Satisfies) by the same author and also dealing with prayer is inserted. The kitab *Munyat al-Musallî* (The Book of the Desire of the Prayer), a thirty-seven page book, was completed in Mecca 1242 A.H. (1826/7 A.D.), while the *al-Bahjah al-Mardîyah*, a five page treatise, was also finished in Mecca in 1259 A.H. (1842/3 A.D.). It was later printed by Dar al-Ma'arif, Penang, Malaysia.

Kitab *Sullam al-Mubtadi' fî-Ma'rifat Ṭarîqat al-Muhtadî*

This book discusses the sources of religious doctrine according to the opinions of the orthodox Muslims of *ahl al-sunnah wa-al-jamâ'ah*. It also discusses the precepts of jurisprudence in general. Shaykh Dawud finished compiling and translating this forty-seven page book in Mecca in 1252 A.H. (1836/7 A.D.). It was revised by al-Hajj Ilyas Yaqub al-Azhari, and first printed at Dâr Iḥyâ' al-Kutub al-'Arabîyah, Cairo, Egypt. This edition was later reprinted by Dar al-Ma'arif, Penang, Malaysia. This book has been extensively commented upon and explained in *Kitâb Kifâyat al-Muhtadî* by Muhammad Nur bin Muhammad bin Isma'il al-Fatani who started writing this 377 page book in Mecca, finishing it in Medina in 1252 A.H. (1836/7 A.D.).

Kitâb *Iḍâḥ al-Bâb li-Murîd al-Nikâḥ bi-al-Ṣawâb*

In the introduction to this book, Shaykh Dawud states in Arabic:

> This is a small commentary, covering the law and the rule of marriage. It concerns also divorce and what is involved, as well as the other things necessary for those who need to know the right way of marriage. I compiled this book depending on the books of the respected (Shafi'ite) *madhhab* such as *Minhâj al-Ṭâlibîn* (by Muḥyî al-Dîn al-Nawâwî), *Fatḥ al-Wahhâb* (by Shaykh Zakariya al-Ansari), *Tuḥfat al-Muḥtâj* (by Shihâb al-Dîn Aḥmad ibn Ḥajar), *al-Nihâyah* (by Shihab al-Din Muhammad al-Ramli), *al-'Uddah wa-al-Silâḥ* (by Muhammad ibn Ahmad). I entitled this book *Iḍâḥ al-Bâb li-Murîd al-Nikâḥ bi-al-Ṣawâb* (The Clarifying Chapter for Him Who Desires to Know the Right Way of Marriage).
>
> (Shaykh Dawud al-Fatani)

The compiler and translator finished this sixty page work in Mecca in 1224 A.H. (1808/9 A.D.). It was revised by Uthman Salih al-Azhari and first published by Dâr Iḥyâ' al-Kutub al-'Arabîyah, Cairo, Egypt. This edition was reprinted by Dar al-Maarif, Penang, Malaysia.

Kitâb *Kifâyat al-Muhtâj*

This book discusses the *isra* and *mir'aj*, the journey by night from Mecca to Jerusalem and the ascension of the Prophet to the highest heaven. In the margins of this twenty-seven page treatise, the story about the Prophet and others is inserted. This work has been rendered into Jawi from the Risalah of Najm al-Dîn al-Ghaytî and some commentaries by Ahmad Shihab al-Din. It was completed in 1224 A.H. (1808/9 A.D).

Shaykh Ahmad bin Muhammad Zayn bin Mustafa al-Fatani and His Major Works
Kitâb Farîdat al-Farâ'id fî 'Ilm al-'Aqâ'id

This twenty-four page book discusses the *'ilm al-tawhîd* based on the *madhhab* of the Imam al-Ashari. Shaykh Ahmad, after having begun with the traditional Islamic invocation, praising Allah and praying for the Prophet Muhammad, introduced his work in Arabic, thus:

> This is a treatise on the science of al-tawhid (the study of the Unity of God) in which I gathered from several well-regarded books, picking up tasty fruits and precious jewels from its ponds... according with the Asharite *madhhab,* in the Malay language, Patani in expression, with clear explanations... I entitled this book *Farîdat al-Farâ'id fî-'Ilm al-'Aqâ'id* (The Precious Gem of Gems in the Science of Creeds). Upon Allah I rely, and His bounty I seek.
>
> (Shaykh Ahmad al-Fatanî)

The book was completed in Mecca in 1313 A.H. (1895/6 A.D.). It was revised by Uthman Salih al-Azhari and first printed at Dâr Ihyâ' al-Kutub al-'Arabîyah, Cairo, Egypt. This edition was reprinted by Dar al-Maarif, Penang, Malaysia.

Bahjat al-Mubtadîn wa-Farhat al-Mujtadîn

This sixty-three page book discusses *'ilm usûl al-dîn* and *fiqh* (jurisprudence) relating to ritual obligations (ibadat) and social relationships. In the margins of this book, certain explanations and commentaries by the author were added. Shaykh Ahmad, in his forward in Arabic says:

> This is a small pamphlet which was compiled quickly and in abbreviated form about the principles of Islamic law and its branches. And a moistener with which beginners can moisten themselves before entering the ponds of its water-sources. It is a cut-piece of gold with which they can ornament themselves before they dressed themselves in necklaces of gems and a snack they enjoy before sitting at the dinner tables. It is the first delicious fruits of the season, and most highly revered of their splendid writings... I named this pamphlet *Bahjat al-Mubtadîn wa-Farhat al-Mujtadîn* (The Delight of the Beginners and Pleasure of Those Who Seek Answers) with a hope that it will be helpful for the young students as well as directing to it the desires of all those who are interested. May Allah accept our prayer.
>
> (Shaykh Ahmad al-Fatani)

This book was completed in Mecca in 1310 A.H. (1892/3 A.D.); and printed at al-Matba'ah al-Mîrîyah, Mecca. The seventh edition was revised by the author's son, Ismail Ahmad and was reprinted by Dar al-Maarif, Penang, Malaysia.

Kitab *Abniyat al-Asmâ' wa-al-Af'âl*

This book is followed by *al-Risâlah al-Fatânîyah*. The former is a discussion of Arabic morphology with special emphasis on nouns (*asmâ'*) and verbs (*af'âl*), while the latter, that is, *al-Risâlah al-Fatânîyah*, discusses the grammar (*nahw*) in more general terms ranging from the sections on the parts of speech and what concerns it (*al-kalâm wa-mâ yata 'allaqu bihi*), to the section on conjunction (*al-'atf*), written in meters and rhymes. Shaykh Ahmad suggests that the beginner should memorize it and learn it before any thing else, so that he will reach his target and fulfil the aims of the author. This book consists of thirty-eight pages and is written in Arabic. According to Muhammad al-Zahrî al-Ghamrâwî, the head of the revision committee of Matba'at Dâr al-Kutub al-'Arabîyah, Cairo, Egypt, the book was first printed by Matba'at al-Kamâlîyah, Kota Bharu, Kelantan, Malaysia. This was at the end of Dhû al-Hijjah 1355 A.H. (1935/6 A.D.). This edition has been reprinted by Dar al-Maarif, Penang, Malaysia.

Kitab *al-Fatâwá al-Fatânîyah*

This book contains several questions and answers. These questions and answers are provided by the late Shaykh Ahmad as a response to the religious problems to which solutions were sought by the Muslims from Patani, as well as those from neighbouring countries like Cambodia and Malaysia and regional communities such as that of Kelantan, an east-coast state of Malaysia. The 220 page-long book was printed under the sponsorship of Nik Abdul al-Rashid bin Idris with the permission of the author's son, Wan Ismail Ahmad.

Kitab *Sufi and Waliyullah*

As with the heritage of Shaykh Ahmad, this book has been revised and reedited by Ustadh Wan Muhammad Saghir Abd Allah and published by Pustaka Aman Press, Kota Bharu, Kelantan. This 138 pages book is divided into five chapters. Chapter one discusses the meaning of mysticism (tasawwuf). Its benefits and several terms of tasawwuf are discussed. Chapter two concerns the answers to the questions asked by Putra Sultan Muhammad, the Sultan of Kelantan. In Chapter three, Shaykh Ahmad arranged his writings in the form of poetic advice, relating to the development of *tasawwuf* and the *tariqah* (mystical path) which occured during his time. Some of his poetically rhymed advice flows in the stream of Patani Malay dialect in a section entitled "Shair Nasihat" where Malay is mingled with Arabic Islamic terms. In Chapter four Shaykh Ahmad speaks about the *wali* (friend of Allâh, saint) and *karamah* (a miracle worked by a saint). In this chapter, he included the names of some well-known *Sufis* and their commitments to the world of Sufism; persons such as Sidi (Sayyidi) Ahmad Rifai, Sidi Shaykh

Abd al-Qadir al-Jilani, Sidi Ahmad al-Badawi, Sidi Ibrahim al- Dusuqi and Sidi al-Shaykh Abu al-Hassan al-Shadhili. In Chapter five, the last chapter of the book, he reminds his Muslim brothers to consider the results of their lives. He asks them to ponder the past glory of all the great ancient states that history has then recorded: all of them, at last, coming to an end unable to escape from declining point. He gives to this chapter the subtitle of *kata-kata nasihat dan hikmah,* a Malay expression meaning advice and wisdom.

Kitab *Ṭîb al-Iḥsân fî-Ṭibb al-Insân*

The title of this sixty-three pages book indicates that it contains the discussion of medical prescriptions. Besides being an Islamic scholar in the Malay Muslim World, Shaykh Ahmad essayed to produce an important work dealing with the medicines derived from local natural plant resources that flourish in the soil of the Malay lands, the *bumi Melayu,* because he was surprised to find his people neglecting such important herbal practices. He strongly hopes that his new generations, whose aspirations were so high, would seriously take part in medicinal research aimed at discovering the secrets of the herbs. Shaykh Ahmad collected this information on the medical uses of plants on several books (the author did not mention the names of the books) and translated them into Malay. He also took them from the mouths of those respected Malays whose information he believed were trustworthy. Above all, he gained this knowledge from the teacher under whom he studied and obtained a certificate of qualification. Shaykh Ahmad finished drafting this work in 1312 A.H. (1894/5 A.D.)

Kitab *Luqṭat al-'Ajalân fîmâ Tamussu ilayhî Ḥâjat al-Insân*

This book deals with phsyco-medical treatments based on the Quranic verses and some secret names of Allah. It discusses the moral virtue of prayer (doa) and supplications (selawat) and also the talisman, amulets that are transmitted by tradition (ma'thûr). This thirty-page book, divided into ten chapters, was finished in 1301 A.H. (1883/4 A.D.). It was first published by Persama Press, Penang, Malaysia in 1368 A.H. (1948/9 A.D.).

Shaykh Zayn al-Abidin bin Muhammad al-Fatani and His Major Works
Kitab *Kashf al-Lithâm 'an As'ilat al-Anâm*

This treatise on Islamic jurisprudence, 407 pages in length, is divided into two parts, the second of which begins with the Kitab *al-Farâ'id* (inheritance law). To make this book more complete, the Kitab *Wishâḥ al-Afrâḥ wa-Isbâḥ al-Falâḥ* (The book of the Sash of Joy and the Light of Victory) by Shaykh

Muhammad bin Ismail Dawud al-Fatani was copied into the margins. Shaykh Zayn al-Abidin, after praising Allah and invoking blessing on the Prophet Muhammad (peace be upon him), begins his introduction by telling us that this work was done at the request of his friends, who were in need of knowing about Islamic precepts written in Jawi, the Arabic script form of the Malay language. He includes his hopes that the work will offer guidance for all and that it will help in solving their problems. This book is printed by Sulayman Mari Press, Singapore.

Kitab *Aqîdat al-Nâjîn fî-'Ilm Uṣûl al-Dîn*

The author translated this book on the sources of Islamic law mainly from the *muqaddimah* of Shaykh Sanusi. The discussion in this book of 140 pages is based on the *madhhab* of orthodox Muslims of *ahli al-sunnah wa-al-jama'ah*. The author completed this book in 1308 A.H. (1890/1 A.D.). It was revised by al-Hajj Ilyas Yaqub al-Azhari and was first printed by Dâr Iḥyâ al-Kutub al-Arabîyah in Cairo, Egypt. The fourth edition was published by Dar al-Maarif, Penang, Malaysia, with the permission of the author's son Shaykh Hasan ibn Zayn al-Abidin, also known as Tuan Minal.

Kitab *Kashf al-Ghaybîyah*

At the begining of this book, the author after praising Allah and praying for the Prophet Muḥammad, said:

This is a treatise (containing material) I found in *Daqâ'iq al-Akhbâr fî-Dhikr al-Jannah wa-al-Nâr* by Imam Abd al-Rahim ibn Ahmad al-Qadi and *al-Durar al-Ḥisân* by al-Suyuti and *Mashâriq al-Anwâr* by Shaykh Hasan al-Adwi as well as others. I translated them into the Jawi tongue for those who don't know Arabic and I named this book *Kashf al-Ghaybîyah fî-Aḥwâl Yaum al-Qiyâmah* (Lifter of the Unseen Concerning the Situations of the Resurrection Day). I hope that it will be made purely for the sake of Allah, dedicating its reward to the soul of the great master (Muhammad).

(Shaykh Zayn al-Fatani)

This book is divided into ten chapters dealing with such topics as the creation of the soul and Nur Muhammad, the creation of Adam, and the virtue of heaven and its people. The compilation and translation of the 152 pages book was finished in the year 1301 of the Hijrah (1883/4 A.D.). It was revised by al-Hajj Ilyas Yaqub al-Azhari and was first published by Dâr Iḥyâ al-Kutub al-'Arabîyah in Cairo, Egypt. This edition has been reprinted by Dar al-Maarif, Penang, Malaysia.

Kitab *Irshâd al-Ibâd ilâ Sabîl al-Rashâd*

This is a booklet of only twenty pages. It was written by Shaykh Zayn al-Abidin who was also known as Tuan Minal. The book is aimed at bringing believers into the right path, that is, the way of the orthodox Muslims of the *ahli al-sunnah wa-al jamâ'ah* who have followed the way of the Prophet Muhammad and the Four Rightly Guided Caliphs (*al-Khulafâ' al-Râshidûn*) without an admixture of (disapproved) innovation in practice (bidah).

There is no indication showing where and when the book was written, but the colophon notes that the book was revised by Uthman Salih al-Azhari. Similarly, there is no clue as to the book was first published, but the edition noted here shows that the book was printed by Dar al-Marif, Penang, Malaysia.

Kitab *Miftâh al-Murîd fî-Ilm al-Tawhîd*

This treatise is also written by Shaykh Zayn al-Abidin (Tuan Minal) whose pure intention, he writes, is to have the Malay Muslims of Patani become acquainted with the *'ilm al-tawhid* (the doctrine of the Unity of God), especially the attributes of Allâh. We find in this sixteen pages treatise, besides the work of Shaykh Zayn al-Abidin, essays by two other writers, one of whom is the author's son Umar, who wrote about the causes that lead to apostasy, *murtadd*. The other is Haji Ahmad Melaka who composed his essay in a type of Malay rhyme. The book was revised by Hajj Ilyas Yaqub al-Azhari and this edition is printed by Dar al-Maarif, Penang, Malaysia.

Muhammad bin Ismail Dawud al-Fatani and His Major Works *Matla' al-Badrayn wa-Majma' al-Bahrayn*

This 235 page book is very famous. It explains the pillars of Islam and faith (iman). It also discusses the science of the Unity of God (*'ilm al-tawhid*) and the science of jurisprudence (*'ilm al-fiqh*). Muhammad Ismail Dawud al-Fatani introduced his book in Arabic saying:

My father asked me to collect for him something of the virtues of knowledge and the religious creeds, and that I added to that some essential things from the *fiqh* chapters translated into our language, so as to bring both of them near to our minds. I obeyed his command, hoping that it would bring some good. I compiled here abstracts of several problems [*masâ'il*] from many well-regarded books, all of which are gleamed from their pearls and are credited to them. So, what is found correct in it, is what is hidden in them and what is stored in them. What is found wrong, is from the slipping of my pen in composing some of its expressions. It is requested of those who read it that they kindly make corrections in it and erase the slips .... I named this book *Matla' al-Badrâyn wa-Majma' al-Bahrâyn* 'The Rising Place of the Two Full Moons' and 'The Joining of the Two Seas'. May God make it pure for His sake. There is neither might nor power but in God, the Most High and the Most Exalted.

(Muhammad al-Fatani)

This book was completed in Mecca in 1303 A.H. (1885/6 A.D.), and revised by al-Hajj Ilyas Yaqub al-Azhari. This edition was printed by Dar Maarif, Penang, Malaysia.

Kitab *Wishâh al-Afrâh wa-Isbâh al-Falâh*

This sixty-four page book (The Embroidered Sash of Joys and Dawning of Success) explains the five pillars of Islam and faith (iman) along with some Hadith about the punishment of those who abandon the practice of ritual prayer. It also places particular emphasis on the laws regarding ritual purity, and gives details of cleansing procedures for all types of impurity (Muhammad al-Fatani undated P1). The author completed the treatise in Mecca in 1312 A.H. (1894/5 A.D.). It was revised by al-Hajj Ilyas Yaqub al-Azhari, and published by Matba'at Dâr Ihyâ' al-Kutub al-`Arabîyah, Cairo, Egypt. This edition was reprinted by Dâr al-Maarif, Penang, Malaysia.

CHAPTER 3

The Patani Ulama and their Roles in Islamic Education

Writing, Translating, Teaching and Publishing

Following the brief study of the valuable work of the four leading ulama of Patani in the previous chapter, one may begin to understand that the ulama of Patani, through men such as these, have performed a great service that has never yet been equaled nor indeed surpassed by any generation of Patani scholars who have succeeded them nor have their successors been able to produce the same quality and quantity in terms of Islamic textbooks. Their works seem to have embraced and embodied special characteristics of their own in terms of the older, more classical styles and modes of expression. These characteristics might not be quite so familiar to the younger modern Islamic graduates who have never been initiated into the traditional ways of learning. Yet, those who have trained in traditional Islamic learning, either in Patani or in Masjid al-Haram in Mecca, have been granted a great opportunity to read, understand and appreciate classical Islamic Jawi Literature. The ulama of Patani, during the nineteenth century and the second quarter of the twentieth century; men such as Shaykh Dawud al-Fatani, Shaykh Ahmad al-Fatani, Haji Ismail (Pak Do 'Ae) bin Abd. al-Qadir, Bendang Daya, and Haji Ismail (Pak Do 'Ae) bin Haji Wan Ahmad and Tok Semla Tua, used to serve their fellow Malay Muslims in Mecca through teaching generation after generation. In the generation that followed them, in a period that extended from 1920 to 1950 approximately, there were three great ulama of Malay descent known to the Muslims of Patani, who used to teach in the Masjid al-Haram, serving their fellow Muslims in religious education. One of them was Shaykh Abd al-Qadir bin Abd al-Muttalib al-Mandili, an Indonesian, known as Shaykh Qodir. Shaykh Qodir, in the year 1956 to 1957, was assigned the role of rebuttal in debates with Tok Guru Ghani of Pondok Padang Langa from Chana District on the issues of *talqin* and *u ṣallî*. These debates were arranged by the Kaum Tua and Kaum Muda groups (old and new groups), and were held at the Majlis Agama Islam, the building of the Provincial Council for Islamic Affairs, Yala Province.

The other two learned Muslims who used to teach their country men in the Masjid al-Haram, as well as in their homes in Mecca for some years, side by side with Shaykh Qodir, were Haji Ismail bin Abd. al-Qadir, originally from Bendang Daya, Patani, and more commonly known as Pak Do'Ae, and Haji Ismail bin Haji Wan Ahmad, known as Tok Semla Tua. The latter was also known as Pak Do 'Ae, and he no less an active man, continued to teach his students in the Masjid al-Haram as he used to do in Pondok Semla, Patani, before moving to Mecca. Note that these are two individuals who share both the same name and the same nickname, i.e., Ismail and Pak Do 'Ae respectively. To differentiate between the two, Haji Ismail, son of Shaykh Abd al-Qadir form Bendang Daya, Patani is known in Mecca as Pak Do'Ae Mahla, while Haji Ismail, son of Haji Wan Ahmad was widely known as Pak Do 'Ae Semla when he also tought there.

During my research concerning Islamic education in Patani, I had the chance to meet with several religious teachers (tok guru) who used to study under Shaykh Abd al-Qadir bin Abd al-Muttalib al-Mandili, originally from Mandiling, a southern district of North Sumatera, Indonesia, and the two scholars Pak Do 'Ae Semla and Pak Do 'Ae Mahla. One of those religious teachers I met, who was a student of theirs, is Haji Abd al-Rashid bin Haji Tayyib (Chemali) known as Tok Guru Haji Shaed Kok Mee in Pondok Kok Mee, Hat Yai, a Thai-speaking area of Songkla Province.

Before going to Mecca, Tok Guru Haji Shaed studies under Haji Sulong for several years (Pitsuwan 1982). With Haji Sulong he studied Islam and the traditional ways of Islamic thought. He then moved to study under Haji Hasan Pondok Mango who was also the traditional student of Haji Sulong. After spending several years in the search for knowledge under Haji Hasan, Tok Mango, Tok Guru Haji Shaed moved again to study under Pak Do Ae at Pondok Semla and he spent ten years there. Because Pak Do Ae Semla moved to Mecca, some of his former students from Patani, including Haji Shaed, also went to Mecca and they continues studying under his guidance.

Other religious teachers of Patani, besides Haji Abd al-Rashid bin Haji Tayyib, Kok ee, were Haji Idris al-Khayyat bin Haji Wan Ali Bakum and Haji Awang Pondok Cerak Keriang. Haji Idris, who is known as Baba Yeh Tok Jong in Nongchik District, Patani, is the author of Kitab *Thimâr al-Jannah Fi-Tarjumat Risâlat al-Mu'âwanah*. Baba Yeh, who is now teaching at Pondok Tok Jong, Patani, is a contemporary of Tok Guru Haji Awang from Pondok Cerak Keriang, Saiburi, Patani. Both Baba Yeh and Haji Awang used to study in the Masjid al-Haram under Pak Do 'Aes, and Shaykh Abd al-Qadir bin Abd al-Muttalib al-Mandili. These three learned figures of the Malay world attracted a large number of Southeast Asian students whose native tongues were not Arabic.

Time has passed and the old generation has passed away with it. Yet, the present generation has emerged to continue the Islamic teaching which was performed by their illustrious ancestors. With the grace and the blessing of Allah, the teaching of Islam in the Masjid al-Haram in the forms of Jawi-

Arabic intellectual learning is continuing in the traditional style. At the present time it is being conducted by two Muslim intellectuals from Thailand. These two learned gentlemen of Thailand are Haji Ali, known as Kru Li Chaiya, and Haji Husayn, known as Kru Sen Surat. Both of them originally came from Surat Thani province, a Thai-speaking area in the south of Thailand. Kru Li Chaiya serves his fellow Muslims from Thailand by teaching them in the Masjid al-Haram, usually employing the Thai language as the medium of interpreting the Arabic texts. Before teaching in the Masjid al-Haram, he taught a number of years in a certain pondok in Waeng District, Narathiwat Province. He was considered by that time to be a well-known figure in the study of comparative religion. Ku Sen Surat, on the other hand, for the most part instructs Muslims from Thailand who use the Malay language as a means of understanding the Arabic texts.

One evening, during both the 'Asr (afternoon) and the Maghrib (after sunset) prayers, I decided to sit in an Islamic learning circle in a corner of the Masjid al-Haram, held by Kru Sen Surat on a regular basis for the seekers of knowledge. In these two periods I found him teaching *Tafsîr al-Jalâlayn* and *al-Iqnâ* dealing with Quranic interpretation and Islamic jurisprudence respectively. I found his method of teaching to be typical of that followed by the religious teacher in the traditional Islamic institutions (pondok) of Patani. He first read the Arabic texts with the translation in Malay and then restated the texts while analysing the grammatical structures in order to make sure that the students comprehended the text (*matn*). The students jotted down what they heard from their teacher, writing explanations, translations and information on other sources underneath the lines of the Arabic text and in the margins. I gained a comprehensive impression of what he has been doing and found myself hoping that there would be learned Muslims from the Malay-speaking lands who would continue the heritage of such traditional teaching, so that the learning that forges links between Patani and Mecca will last forever.

On one fine occasion during the late evening, on my way back to my quarters and while walking up the foothill from the Masjid al-Haram, together with Kru Sen Surat and some friends from southern Thailand, I asked him whether there is a student who is currently able to serve as a teaching assistant and ultimately to take over his work when the time comes. He seemed to say, in so many words, "God knows best" (Interview in Masjid al-Haram 1979).

Masjid al-Haram is the most blessed center of Islamic teaching. The most devout Muslims of Thailand hope to send their children to study under its roof; to sit under certain religious mentors acquiring Islamic knowledge for a number of years. In act, every corner of the Masjid al-Haram is being used for circles (*halaqât*) of Islamic study. The seekers of knowledge are free to choose the mentors under whom they would like to sit. It is certainly true that the learning circles at the Masjid al-Haram in Mecca continue to have a great impact upon Muslim, not only those from the Malay Muslim World, but also from every corner of the Muslim community. It is believed that seeking knowledge under the roof of the Masjid al-Haram will bring blessing (barakat). Traditionally therefore, the Muslims of Thailand in particular, harbour hopes to continue their study in Mecca, to sit under certain teachers for a period of perhaps years. C. Snouck Hurgronje confirms that the peculiar blessing (barakah) of the place is supposed to rest on knowledge acquired in the holiest mosque on earth (Hurgronje 1931). The act of sitting and studying under teachers is itself also regarded as obtaining *barakah* or blessing.

The Malay Muslims of Thailand usually come to study in the Masjid al-Haram during the time of the <u>hajj</u>. Besides trying to find opportunities to study, they also perform the <u>hajj</u>, the fifth pillar of Islam. If the situation permits them to stay longer in Mecca, they may continue to sit under certain teachers, year after year, until they really become initiated into traditional Islamic learning. The process of learning of non-Arabic speaking groups in the Masjid al-Haram is clearly described by C. Snouck Hurgronje who remarks:

The great majority of the students come from abroad, and if their mother tongue is not Arabic, must go through long preliminary study in that language before they are ripe for instruction in the Haram. Few have attained in their Javanese, Malay, Malabar, or other home such a knowledge of Arabic as to enable them to follow the lectures; most come very young of very imperfectly prepared in that respect. In such cases, after having made some progress in reciting the Qur'ân, they go for some years to school to a learned fellow-country man living in Mecca, who explains to them the easier texts in their mother tongue.

(Hurgronje 1931)

Hurgronje says that these students, after having overcome such difficulties, might sit under such native learned teachers for some more years, 'the more so because there are among the foreign scholars (many) not inferior to their Arab colleagues' (1931). These Jawa people are both teachers and students. Hurgronje says:

In Mecca, they are the ones most highly regarded: from their country folk on pilgrimage they enjoy the deepest awe, and from Mecca they control the religious life of their homes. Almost all Jawa who teach in the Holy City have risen to this height in Mecca herself.

(Hurgronje 1931)

It should be noted that under the term Jawa, as it is used by Hurgronje, are included all people of Malay race in the fullest meaning of the term; the geographical boundary is perhaps from Siam and Melaka to New Guinea.

In the mean time, the Muslim communities back home are waiting to see them return, highly qualified with knowledge. The Muslim communities usually prepare to welcome them with parcels of donated land (*awqâf*) and build them Islamic centers for traditional teaching, as they did for their former teachers.

The reader may recall from our survey of the major works of the Patani ulama that most of their writings were written while they were in Mecca. During this time, they had established good relationships with Muslim intellectuals of the Near East and especially those in the Holy Cities, in Egypt and the educational authorities, as well as those who came from the Malay Muslim lands. Through the latter, they built a cordial connection with the *Muslim communities of Southeast Asia, the seekers of knowledge (tullâb al-'ilm)*, as well as the authorities who involved themselves in the printing process. The Patani ulama in Mecca established a strong link with their communities back home via those religious students who came to study under them. Their excellent qualifications in Islamic subjects had drawn the enthusiastic attention of those that were interested in seeking knowledge. The pattern can be traced back to Shaykh Ahmad who had a great influence on the Malay-Muslim community to extent to which he attracted many pupils from the Malay-speaking world.

Among those who later became famous were Nik Mahmud bin Nik Ismail who studied politics with Shaykh Ahmad and became Prime Minister of Kelantan, Haji Ibrahim who became Chief Mufti of Kelantan, Shaykh Mahmud Sa'id who became Senior Mufti of Negeri Sembilan, Khatib Jabar, later the Maharaja Imam of Sambas (West Kalimantan), Haji Muhd. Salih who became Chief Kadi and others who established (a) pondok, or became religious teachers in Patani and Malaysia.

(Matheson & Hooker 1988)

There is no doubt that, among other important things, Kelantan and Patani are strongly tied together by the joint heritage of traditional education which has brought about deeply-rooted connections through the religious ulama of both areas.

Indeed, the ties between Kelantan and Patani, political and economic as well as religious, continue to be important. Important religious leaders in Kelantan not uncommonly trace their families to Patani and it is thus not unlikely that the traditional schools derive at some point from this area as well.

(Winzeler 1975)

The strong spiritual relationship that has always linked Kelantan and Patani is exemplified by religious leaders like Muhammad Yusuf, locally known as To'Kenali (b. 1866, d.1933), who in 1886, at the age of twenty, went to Mecca, and in 1903 he went to Egypt with two Patani scholars to visit the

Azhar and other educational institutions. (Johns 1981). Furthermore, we learn that:

Another well-known Kelantan teacher, Haji Wan Musa b. Haji Abd al-Samad (b.1874) who was taken by his father to Mecca while still a child, with three of his brothers. Among his teachers in Mecca was the same Wan Ahmad al-Fatani who was the teacher of To'Kenali and with whom he studied jurisprudence and scholastic theology.
(Johns 1981)

Reliable sources also indicate that the ideas of Islamic reform in the Muslim community held by To'Kenali and Haji Nik Mahmud bin Haji Nik Ismail have been taken from this teacher, Haji Wan Ahmad bin Muhammad Zayn bin Mustafa al-Fatani who liked to discuss politics (Nik Hassan 1983). It is certain that the influence of the Patani ulama such as him upon the Kelantan ulama, through writing and thought, has been widespread. The religious books of the Patani ulama have been and are read and used in Kelantan as textbooks. Confirming this, Nik Abdul Aziz bin Nik Hassan, the author of the *Sejarah Perkembangan* Ulama *Kelantan,* (Historical Development of the Kelantan Ulama also poses a rhetorical question on the subject:

If the kitab (religious books) which are written by the ulama of Patani, such as those that were written by Shaykh Dawud al-Fatani, Haji Wan Ahmad bin Muhammad Zayn bin Mustafa al-Fatani are strongly received and accepted in the District of Kota Bharu, Kelantan and furthermore, each of the educational systems of the pondok depends upon the books written by them; what are the geographical factors then, that caused such a situation. This question calls for further deep research.
(Nik Abdul Aziz 1983)

In terms of being a politically-minded person of some manner, Shaykh Ahmad assumed a strong and prominent role in dealing with foreign authorities whether it was concerning a political problem or an educational issue. Here we find that:

Shaykh Ahmad had an ambition to see the establishment of a Malay Islamic Kingdom which would stretch from south Patani to Kelantan and Terengganu. He even approached Turkey to give aid and support to Kelantan so that it could resist Siamese control and come under British protection. He also had contact with Cham Muslims in Cambodia whom he urged to set up their own state. He advised the Cham to study in Patani or Kelantan first before travelling to Mecca.
(Matheson & Hooker 1988)

It is recorded by Snouck Hurgronje, writing in *Mecca in the Latter Part of the 19th Century,* that Shaykh Ahmad was a well-qualified figure in Islamic literature, to the extent that he was honored by the Turkish authority with the charge of the printing press producing Malay Islamic books Hurgronje says:

The Turkish Government (in 1884) has entrusted a certain Ahmed ibn Muhammed Zein from Patani (Malacca) with the supervision of the Malay Press. To this is probably due to the fact that the works of divines from Patani are most numerously represented in the Mecca editions. This Ahmad is a savant of merit.

(Hurgonje 1931)

It is a fact that in those days the Patani ulama as well as their works were highly valued by the Mecca authorities. Hurgronje mentioned that the Rector Ahmed Dahlan claimed in his chronicle of the town of Mecca:

That the Printing Press of the Holy City, founded at the behest of the reigning Sultan, over tops all others in that here apart from Arabic and Turkish, also Malay books can be printed. But one must admit that, bearing in mind the short life of this press and the Turkish leisure which characterizes most of its activities, the Malay Literature takes a place of honor among its productions.

(Hurgronje 1931)

The far-sighted Patani ulama considered the role of printing so important that they worked to establish a good permanent relationship with the personnel of those presses in Cairo and Mecca that specialized in publishing classical Arabic and Islamic works. As a result of these personal and scholarly relationships, most of their books were revised by graduates of al-Azhar University as shown by the *nisbah* "al-Azharî" attached to their names, as found in both al-Hajj Illyas Yaqub al-Azhari and Uthman Salih al-Azhari who took an important part as the revisers of the Kitab Jawi.

It is very important to remark here that, in those days, there were strong links to the Muslim educational institutions created by the Patani ulama in the form of direct contact between Mecca and the Malay-Muslim World via Cairo. Beside Mecca, Cairo in those days used to serve as a printing center for the Jawi Islamic literature written by the ulama of Patani while they were in Mecca.

Through the examination of the Kitab Jawi written by the ulama of Patani, we find that Matba'at Dar Ihyâ' al-Kutub al-'Arabîyah of Cairo, Egypt, whose owner (Malay: *kepunyaan*) at that time was 'Isá al-Bâbî al-Halabî wa-Shurakâ'uh, was playing an important role in supplying and distributing the Jawi Islamic literature to the Malay-Muslim World and the Malay Muslim community of Patani in particular. This direct contact between the Cairo printing press and Patani is still evident up to this date. The evidence can be easily found in a document in the form of a receipt issued on June 15, 1986 by Moustafa El-Baby El-Halaby & Sons, Publishers Printers and Bookbinders to al-Sayyid Muhammad Nahdi, the owner of Muhammad Nahdi Bookstore in the downtown area of Patani. Muhammad Nahdi is also the owner of the Maktabat wa-Matba'at Dâr al-Ma'ârif in Penang, Malaysia. Muhammad Nahdi is the only distributor of Patani who still keeps in touch with the Middle Eastern printing business, especially with the Cairo printing house mentioned here. Muhammad Nahdi still orders certain major important Arabic books on *fiqh, uṣûl al-fiqh, tafsîr, naḥw, ḥadîth* and *taṣawwuf*, as well as other, modern types of Arabic books for the *madrasah* systems.

The Arabic Influence Among the Muslim Community of Patani

The Influence of the Kitab Jawi

As far as the Arabic definition previously given in this work is concerned, I once again confirm that the term Arabic in this particular discussion applies to the Arabic language proper as well as to the Jawi Islamic literature written in the Arabic script, known as Jawi writing (tulisan jawi; a Malay writing using Arabic script).

Historically speaking, the writing system of the Malay language, which dates back to the seventh century was quite different from its counterpart today. It is believed that:

The ancient inscription stones found in Sumatera and Bangka indicated that the writing system of Malay was adopted from the Indian Pali script, an evidence of Hindu-Buddhist influence in the area during that time.

(Madmarn 1982)

This ancient system of writing was then almost totally replaced by the Arabic script, due to the spreading of Islamic influence into the regions.

With the Islamization of the Malay Peninsular in the thirteen century, Islam brought with it the message of the Quran and its script. Thus, abandoning original Indian script, the Malays adopted the Arabic writing system with certain modifications to suit the local phonological system.

(Madmarn 1982)

In studying the Kitab Jawi written by the ulama of Patani mentioned above, we find that the Arabic language plays the prime role conveying Islamic knowledge to the Muslims in the Malay Peninsular and Patani Muslims in particular. This is because most of the Kitab Jawi are concerned directly with Islamic teachings and are largely translated from the major Arabic books, as I have remarked earlier. In translation, the ulama of Patani, by and large, retained the major Islamic terms and terminology in the original Arabic so as to bring the attention of students to such important words in the Arabic contexts. Thus, the students learn both the Arabic and as a means of comprehending the Islamic and Arabic texts.

Most of the Kitab Jawi written by the four leading ulama of Patani previously introduced are well-known to the Muslims community of Thailand

and are used as study works fundamental to the understanding of Islamic precepts (*al-aḥkâm al-shar'îyah*). These books are still being read and taught in the Muslim community to both Malay and Thai-speaking groups. The well-versed traditionally oriented Muslims of Thailand use this books as their major guides and reference when religious problems (*masâ'il khilâfiyah*) occur. They read these books mostly in the libraries (the attached-wall bookshelves) of the mosque and in the *balaisah*, a smaller prayer house. Through these Kitab Jawi, the traditional Muslims students of Thailand also learn how to understand certain segments of the Arabic texts. So important is the function of the Kitab Jawi that there is no indication that either the Kitab Jawi or their use will disappear from the Muslim community in the foreseeable future.

I once asked Muhammad Nahdi, the owner of Muhammad Nahdi Bookstore in Patani, about the attitude of the Malay Muslims of Patani towards the Kitab Jawi. His answer was that the Kitab Jawi was the best sellers in the store. Though the traditional institutions, the pondok have been physically transformed into new structures and the system of education has adopted modern methods of teaching, the need of Kitab Jawi is no less than what it was in past decades. The Kitab Jawi are being used and read by the students of the modern schools (madrasah) and the traditional students as well as adults who are no longer in the school system.

The students of the madrasah system usually read the Kitab Jawi during the evening hours. It is most likely that they read the Kitab Jawi before or after the Maghrib (after sunset) and Isyak (evening) prayers, since they are usually busy with the study program of the school system during the day. The Kitab Jawi, in fact, are specifically serving those who have little background in understanding the original Arabic texts. The concepts embodied in and conveyed through the Kitab Jawi have penetrated deeply, rooting themselves into the Malay-Muslim community of Patani, not only among a group which might be classified as fairly well-educated and incorporating those who used to be oriented to these things through the traditional system of learning, no indeed merely among those who have graduated from institutions organized on more modern lines, but also amongst the common people who acquire Islamic knowledge through a more informal type of education.

This group learns the Islamic precepts from the Kitab Jawi, which are taught either by the learned man in the village, the imam, or by the religious teachers of the pondok. This type of informal education that is individually organized, is a life long process by which everyone acquires knowledge, skills and attitudes through experience and through contact with other to provide an important foundation for the understanding of Islam (Haddad 1980). Through this process, Muslims in the community learn at least how to read the necessary Quranic verses involved in the daily ritual prayers of formal worship (solat) and some of the other recommended Arabic lines for orison and supplication (doa and ibtihal).

The Kitab Jawi and the Arabic Language

Before the coming of the Western colonialist, Jawi was the only writing system used in the Malay communities. When the colonial powers came to the Malay Peninsular in the sixteenth century, beginning with the conquest of Melaka by the Portuguese in 1511, the Dutch in 1641 and the British in 1795, the natives came in contact with Western culture, which were generally limited to trading activities. Through this largely commercial contact, the Latin alphabet may possibly have been introduced to the Malay community. There is however, a great uncertainty as to early impact of these colonial powers upon the Malay writing system, since the romanized Malay was introduced into the Malay elementary schools and taught side by side with Jawi only from the beginning of the twentieth century (Ongkili 1985). Later on, the Malay population began to exert pressure on the government to make Malay the sole official language.

Led by (the late) Syed Nasir bin Ismail, the Director of the Dewan Bahasa dan Pustaka (Language and Literature Agencies) the Malays set up in early 1965 a *Barisan Bertindak Bahasa Kebangsaan* (*his*) or 'National Language Action Front' to assist the government in the implementation of Malay (romanized Malay) as the official language by 1967.

(Ongkili 1985)

The romanized Malay in fact became the official language when the National Language bill was passed in March 1967. The first introduction of the Latin alphabet into Indonesian societies, however may have taken place earlier, though it is true that many natives are familiar with other alphabets for example, in Western Jawa and Madura the Arabic alphabets is used, since the religious texts are written in it (Robequain 1958). Besides the writing system, the problem of the language to be used as a medium was one of the most difficult that faced the colonial education system. The following questions were always raised among the colonizing nations:

What language should be used for the native inhabitants who form the great bulk of school children? Shall it be their mother tongue, a language commonly used in business matters, or the language of the metropolitan country? The native tongues are many, but they are often unsuitable for expressing abstract or scientific ideas and their use would greatly complicate education.

The outcome of such complicated considerations can be inferred from a remark of Syed Naquib al-Attas:

In the Archipelago, the coming of Western imperialism as well as the imposition of western culture beginning in 10th/16th century certainly seem to have interrupted and retarded the process of Islamization.

In fact, the introduction of the Latin alphabet for writing Malay and transliterating Arabic for the Muslim community has appeared to have a negative impact upon the Muslim youth. This change impoverishes the peoples knowledge of the fundamentals of the Arabic language, especially that of the Quran and thus introducing difficulties for the Muslim youth in reciting the Quran and grasping its subtleties for the Latin forms do not represent the Arabic precisely. Syed Naquib confirms that "the appearance of the Europeans on the Malay-Indonesian scene and their control over the area have left their effects upon the Muslim" (Naquib al-Attas 1969).

To read the Kitab Jawi, one has to be knowledgeable in the classical Malay language and must also be acquainted to a substantial degree with the Arabic language and the four skills of listening, reading, writing and speaking it, for passages in the Arabic language are quoted as texts or are referred to and serve as the source material around which the discussions in the Kitab Jawi are centered. These texts are aimed mainly at supporting the arguments and thereby justifying answers or conclusions concerning religious problems (*masâ'il shar'îyah*) occurring during the discussions. In some certain cases, the fatwa (authoritative legal opinions), which are given to the Muslim people of Patani as responses to their questions, have been totally expressed through the Arabic language. Yet, a translation in the Malay language is given so that the Malay Muslims of Patani can understand how these religious problems may be solved.

This Arabic influence among the Muslims of Patani can be seen through the discussions dealing with questions and answers in the book called *al-Fatâwá al-Faṯánîyah* by Shaykh Ahmad bin Muhammad Zayn bin Mustafa al-Fatani. This book offers authoritative legal opinions (*fatwa*) on the religious problems encountered by the Muslim community of Patani and the neighbouring countries. These religious issues involved *masa'il fiqhiyah* (juriprudence problems), *masâ'il al-tawḥîd* (the unity of God), and *masâ'il al-tasawwuf* (mystical issues).

The contents of this book were collected by the author's son, Haji Wan Ismail Ahmad, who also acted as the Arabic-Malay translator when the questions were responded to in Arabic. For instance, questions number 22, 23, 48 and 67 in the book were replied to completely in Arabic (Shaykh Ahmad al-Fatani 1958). Out of these questions, questions number 22, 23 and 48 were asked in Arabic while question number 67 was asked in Malay. It is not clearly mentioned how the process of questions and answers was conducted. The process was first conducted through writing. Then, all materials for the questions and answers found in the book were collected and put into published form later. The reason for this is that the solutions to such religious problems must be carefully rendered, especially when quoting the Quranic verses or referring to the Prophetic traditions. For the sake of correctness and to avoid any corruption through vaguery and misinterpretation, the questions and answers must be well-written.

Examining the *al-Fatâwá al-Faṭânîyah* closely, we find that most of the questions and answers are written in Malay using some Arabic terms and sentences, particularly when the evidences (*dalâ'il*) from the Quran and the Hadith are needed to support the given *fatwa*. It is worth mentioning here that the religious problems posited in the book are not confined only to the Muslim brethren of Patani, but also are concerned with others, extending to the Muslims in Cambodia and the Malaysian state of Kelantan. This can be seen from question number 45, 66 and 106 of the book. The first two questions are concerned with the Muslims in Cambodia while the third question is very important, for it is said to have been asked by "the Raja Kelantan, Sultan Muhammad" (Shaykh Ahmad al-Fatani 1958). What is impressive about this is that the ulama of Patani, such as Shaykh Ahmad, are conferred with and consulted upon religious matters by the royal family of Kelantan, who required from him decisive answers. If this indicated something, it is that the ulama of Patani are among the most knowledgeable persons in matters of Islamic doctrine and practice. They are highly respected, not only by their people but also by their neighbours.

Most of the questions that are asked in Arabic usually begin with the words: *"Su'âl: Mâ qaulukum dâma faḍlukum fî..."* (What do you, (God) make your Grace to endure, say concerning...). If the questions are asked in Malay they run *"Apa kata kamu pada..."* In responding to the questions made either in Arabic or Malay, Shaykh Ahmad usually starts with *"al-jawâb, allâhumma hidâyatan lil-ṣawâb."* (The answer, May God guide us into the right path,...) Each answer in usually ended with *"Wa-Allah subḥânahu wa-ta'âlá a'lam,"* which means "God, May He be exalted, knows best." Such aforementioned formula were also found in the Turkish fatwa, which was conventionally;

...introduced in the response by the word *al-ḏjawâb*, 'answer', the characters of which were extended so as to mark a division between what preceded and what followed, the fallibility of all human judgement is immediately acknowledged by the phase *Allâh a'lam* "God knows best".

(Walsh in Lewis et al. 1965)

Reading the book *al-Fatâwá al-Kubrá* of Ibn Taymîyah Abu al-Abas Taqyuddin Ahmad ibn Abd al-Halim, one may find that the styles of asking the questions and responses seemed to be the best model for Shaykh Ahmad in his book *al-Fatâwá al-Faṭânîyah*, for there are several similarities between the two books. It is most likely that Shaykh Aḥmad had read the *al-Fatâwá al-Kubrá* and was profoundly impressed by it. That is to say, most of the questions presented in the *al-Fatâwá al-Kubrá* ended with the words *"Aftûnâ ma'jûrîn"*, as found, for instance, in question number 181, which means "Give us an authoritative opinion, and you are being rewarded." Such a traditional formula is also found in the *al-Fatâwá al-Fatânîyah*; for example, in question number 22. The structures of questions and answers were generally the same although different in particular expression. It should be noted that:

> *The fatwa* document was of a conventional form and varied little over the centuries. It was headed by a pious invocation in Arabic, often written in a very involved and stylized manner and varying from period to period according to the preferences of the drafting clerk; after the middle of 12th - 18th century, however, the formula *al-tawfik minhu*, 'guidance is from Him', became invariable.
>
> (Lewis et al. 1965)

From our previous discussion about various Kitab Jawi of the four leading ulama of Patani, we find that the Arabic language functions largely side by side with its Jawi counterpart. Most of these authors began by expressing their pure intention in the Arabic language in the preface (muqaddimah) of their books. Examples of this have given earlier. We also find in the Kitab Jawi that the Arabic language appears now and then, either in the form of a single word, a phase, or in the form of Quranic verses and Prophetic traditions. More than that, the opinions of the ulama are quoted in a completely Arabic expression and then followed by the explanations. The translation usually conveys a rather literal rendition of Arabic. Within lines of explanations made in Jawi we still find that some Arabic words are left without any attempt at translation. These are invariably those that are technical religious terms defying authoritative translation from the Arabic. By retaining these Arabic terms in the text (Arabic: *matn*) or leaving them untranslated, the author almost certainly intended to teach his Malay readers the Arabic language as well as to expose its structure. By this method, the Malay readers might be acquainted first with the Jawi text and then familiarized with the Arabic one.

Another example of Arabic influence to be mentioned in this context is that found in Shaykh Ahmad's *Tîb al-Ihsân fi Tibb al-Insân*, the book about medical prescriptions described earlier and based on the occurrence of medicinal plants or natural herbal resources found in the Malay environment. Shaykh Ahmad gave the Arabic names of most of the plants herbs as he had come to know them also in the Arabian markets. He then compared them to those that grow in *bumi Melayu* (Malay soil). He tried to identify the plants by describing their features, functions and effectiveness. Shaykh Ahmad based his prescriptions on his experience and referring to what he had learned from his teacher. Besides learning to know the functions and the effectiveness of the plants known by Shaykh Ahmad, we learn also what they were called in Arabic.

Shaykh Ahmad's learning in medical and pharmacological aspects of material is still being read and researched by the current Malay generations, as well as by others, in the constant quest to extent the benefits or such knowledge to all mankind, just as the original author intended.

It is plain that herbal medicine in Patani is still being practiced by Malay Muslim herbalists and is still very popular (Golomb 1985). These respected cures and their forebears have been profoundly influenced over the years by their exposure to the naturalistic etiologies (*ta'lîl al-marad*) of the great traditions of medicine of ancient India, Arabia and China. As a matter of fact, Shaykh Ahmad himself was a student of an Indian physician, Shaykh Abd al-Rahim al-Kabuli.

When we turn to Shaykh Ahmad's psycho-medical book *Luqtat al-'Ajalân*, the contents of which are essentially based on the Quranic verses and the transmitted traditions of the Prophet, we find that there are many words arranged in Arabic, yet the are garbled. This is because some of this Arabic material and even some segments of the Quranic verses have been mixed up with talismanic formula. Louis Golomb (1985) explains that much of the language of a number of those ancient texts has presumably been copied countless times and passed down to us, and even that which is used in accompanying incantations, or in such metaphysical diagnostic techniques as astrology or meditation, is derived from classical India or the Arabic language. However, one may discover that most techniques acquired by Patani-Malay practitioners from their forebears seem to have been transmitted orally or through demonstration rather that in the written Malay/Arabic medium (Golomb 1985).

It should be accepted that the Arabic language performs an important function in every Muslim community in Southeast Asia. Arabic, for them, represents Islam as a religion and religious learning more than a language proper and a literature per se. In reality, in the areas of the world that were Islamicized but were not permanently Arabized (sic), the Arabic language influenced other Muslim languages just as English was greatly influenced by Greek and Latin (Landau 1958). The languages of Muslim Persia and Turkish, Urdu and Swahili, for example, include a large Arabic vocabulary and were once written in the Arabic script.

As we have noted above, in most Muslim communities, children at a very early age are taught to read the Quran prior to anything else. Learning to recite the Quran for them is an act of worship. Muhammad Abdul Jabbar Beg in his book *Arabic Loan-Words in Malay says:*

Arabic is a great cultural language... Arabic is the liturgical language of Islam. The main sources of Islam, al-Quran and al-hadith (traditions), are written in (the) Arabic language. These sources of Islam are read in (the) original Arabic by all Muslims, Arabs as well as non-Arabs, throughout the world. Arabic is the medium of Islam. In other words, Arabic and Islam are intertwined. Arabic loan-words are found in (a) great many languages of Asia, Africa and Europe, e.g., in Asia: Persian, Turkish, Kurdish, Urdu, Hindi, Oriya, Tamil, Bengali, Tibetan, Malay, etc., in Africa: Swahili, Somali, Amharic, Berber, Hausa, etc., in Europe: Spanish, Portuguese, Latin, English, French, Italian, etc.

(Beg 1983)

This shows that all major languages spoken by Muslims in Asia and Africa have adopted Arabic words to express the religious, legal and cultural ideals of Islam. The Muslims of Patani and the nearby areas to a greater or lesser extent, have done the same. They have paid more attention to the Arabic language and the Kitab Jawi, not just because of their deep appreciation in understanding the beauty of the Arabic language nor its sublimity, but because it is the language of the Quran and Islam in the truest sense of the word. They strongly encourage their children to learn how to read the Quran in the hope that they will grow up with some sort of Islamic background, or at least know how to read some Quranic verses equipping them to fulfil the requirements of daily prayers.

In fact, the Arabic language has been an unbreakable thread which has kept the Muslim community of Patani sewn into unity, faith and the fabric of the land since Shaykh Said taught King Phaya Tu Nakpa the *Kalimah Shahadah* the testimony of faith or *kalimah ṯayyibah*. The Arabic phrases, along with their Malay translation, have certainly continued to have a great impact upon the Muslims of Patani ever since. Here, we see the essential religious spirit of Islam... monotheistic, couched in its unique conception of the Unity of God (*al-tawḥîd*). In fact, "Arabic is the language of Islam and no language of any Muslim people, whether or not it has achieved a lofty rank in civilization, is without the profound influence of Arabic." (Naquib al-Attas 1969).

It has been observed that "all the Muslim peoples (have) adopted the Arabic script, creating wherever necessary new letters to represent the phonetic peculiarities not found in Arabic but still basing such letters on the Arabic script" (Naquib al-Attas 1969). Based upon this modified script, which later on turned out to be the Islamized Malay language, in the region concerned here in, were the Kitab Jawi of Patani written and compiled.

Writing about "Religious Actors in Language Spread (1982)," Charles A. Ferguson puts it this way:

The distribution of major types of writing systems in the world correlates more closely with the distribution of the world's major religions than with genetic or typological classifications of language. This correlation between religion and writing systems does not result from any inherent relationship between religious practices or belief and the processes of reading and writing. Rather the present distribution of writing systems is largely a result of the fact that in many instances the spread of a major religion has simultaneously introduced the use of writing into the nonliterate speech community. So it has happened that... wherever Islam has spread to nonliterate communities, it has introduced a variety of the Arabic script for writing previously unwritten languages. Sometimes, when a major religion has spread to a literate community, the effect of the new religion has been to replace a local writing system without replacing the languages spoken in the community, as when the Arabic alphabet replaced the other ways of writing such as Persian or Malay.

(Fergusan 1982).

CHAPTER 4

The Kitab Jawi as the Basic Foundation of Islamic Knowledge

The Products of Patani Ulama and Others

As we have observed, the Kitab Jawi have been written to serve the needs of the Malay Muslims who do not understand the Arabic language. This is what Mohd. Nor bin Ngah says:

> From the early period of Islam in the Malay Archipelago until today, Kitab Jawi have been used by the Malays as a major source of Islamic knowledge because most Malays do not understand Arabic. Abdullah Munshi observed that Arabic was used by the Malays only in worship and prayers.
>
> (Mohd Nor 1982)

Conformation can be seen in the preface of each of the Kitab Jawi written by the four leading Patani ulama that were discussed earlier. That is to say, the pure intention (*nîyah*) of their writing Kitab Jawi is to do so for the sake of Allah and to respond to the repeated requests of their friends whose mother tongue is Malay. Malay is usually referred to in Arabic as lisân al-Jawi by the Kitab Jawi authors that I have already quoted.

The Kitab Jawi that have become the major sources of Islamic knowledge and understanding among the Muslim people of Patani are not only those that were written by the ulama of Patani alone, but also those that were written by other Muslims in various parts of the Malay Muslim world. For instance, the *Sabîl al-Muhtadîn lil-Tafaqquh fi-Amr al-Dîn*, a two-volume book on Islamic law, was written by the Kyai (religious teacher) Shaykh Muhammad Arshad bin Abd Allah al-Banjari. This book is very familiar to the traditional students of Patani and even to the wider spread community of Muslim people of Thailand. Its fame reminds the reader of the hometown from which Kyai Shaykh Muhammad came. That is to say, his last name "al-Banjari" refers to an area of Banjarmasin, the capital city of South Kalimantan, Indonesia. This 206 pages book was written by al-Banjari after he had concluded that *al-Sirât al-Mustaqîm*, a widely used Shafi'ite *fiqh* book by Shaykh Nur al-Din al-Raniri and translated into Jawi, was important but caused difficulties. For some reason, in the *al-Sirât al-Mustaqîm*, certain expressions (ibarat) were transliterated in the Aceh language, making the *al-*

Sirât al-Mustaqîm difficult to comprehend. Also, some expressions are distorted while others are missing, a problem that seems to have developed in the process of transmitting the book. So, in the year 1193 A.H. (1778/9 A.D.) Kyai Shaykh Muhammad Arshad bin Abd Allah al-Banjari was asked to write a book on fiqh based on the Shafi'ite madhhab, rendering this information into the more familiar Jawi writing. He then selected some religious problems (masâ'il) from certain books such as the Sharh al-Manhaj by Shaykh al-Islam Zakariya al-Ansari (1423-1520), Mughnî al-Khatîb by Shirbînî (1570), al-Tuhfah by Ibn Hajar al-Haitamî (ca. 1503-ca. 1565) and from others. He completed the writing on Sunday 27 Rabî' al-Akhîr 1195 A.H 1780/1 A.D. According to the acknowledgment made by Shaykh Ahmad bin Muhammad Zayn al-Fatani, the revisor of the book in the very early work of printing Kitab Jawi, this book was printed first in Mecca and then, according to Shaykh Muhammad Idris al-Marbawi, another revisor, the book was printed by Mustafa al-Bâbî al-Halabî in Dhû al-Hijjah 1343 A.H. (1924/5 A.D.).

There are several books written by Indonesia ulama that have become classics. I would like to mention just three, for each of these books has become a major reference for the traditional students of pondok in Patani. One of these books is the Sirât al-Hudâ by Shaykh Muhammad Zayn al-Din bin Muhammad Nadwi al-Sambawi. This fifty-one page book was aimed at explaining the belief of the pious (ahl al-taqwâ), commenting on the Matn Umm al-Barâhîn of Abu Abd Allah Muhammad ibn Yusuf al-Sanusi. This book was completed in Mecca and revised by Hajj Ilyas Yaqub al-Azhari (al-Sambawi, undated). The second one is Bidâyat al-Hidâyah by Tuan Shaykh Muhammad Zayn bin al-Faqih Jalal al-Din from Aceh. This forty-six page book on fiqh was also written primarily to explain the Matn Umm al-Barâhîn by Imam Sanusi. It was written in the Jawi script for the Jawa people. The book was completed in Mecca on the evening of Juma'ah (Thursday night), 24 Sha'bân 1170 A.H. (1756/7 A.D) (al-Hidayah undated).

The third book by an Indonesian that has been a great influence upon the Muslims of Patani is Kitab Sifat Dua Puluh (the book of twenty attributes). This book was compiled in the year 1304 A.H. (1886/7 A.D.) by Uthman bin Abd Allah bin Yahya from Batavia Jakarta. This twenty-four page book deals with the attributes (sifat) of Allah, explaining them in detail. The names of the attributes are given in Arabic and are followed by explanations in Jawi. This book, as far as the awareness of the 'ilm al-tawhîd (The science of Unity of God) is concerned, has penetrated deeply into the Muslim community, not only in Patani but also throughout Thailand as a whole. The Muslim community, whether from the Malay-speaking group or the Thai speaking community, use this book as the guidelines to understand the 'ilm al-tawhîd. They usually read and discuss

them, as well as memorize some, if not all, of the Islamic terms relating to
the attributes of God.

Twenty attributes are given in Arabic along with the Quranic verses used
as evidences *(dalâ' il)*. They run as follows:

1. Wujud (Existence). He who created the heavens and the earth and all
   that in between, in six days. (Quran 25:59)
2. *Qidam* (Pre-existence). He is the First and the Last, the Immanent and
   Evident. And He has full knowledge of all things. (Quran 57:3)
3. Baqa (Immortality). But will abide (forever) the Face of thy Lord, full
   of Majesty Bounty and Honour. (Quran 55:27)
4. *Mukhalifatuhu ta'âlâ lil-hawâdith.* (His difference from the created
   thing)... there is nothing whatever like unto Him, and He is the One that
   hears and sees (all things). (Quran 42:11)
5. *Qiyâmuhu ta'âlâ bi-nafsihi* (Self-Subsistence). For God is free of all
   needs from all creation. (Quran 29:6)
6. *Wahdânîyah* (Unity). Say He is God, the One Only. (Quran 112:1)
7. *Qudrah* (Capability). For God hath power over all things (Quran 3: 165)
8. *Irâdah* (Will)... for thy Lord is the (sure) Accomplisher of what He
   planneth. (Quran 11: 107)
9. *'Ilm* (Knowledge). And God is well-acquainted with all things. (Quran
   2:282, 9: 115)
10. *Hayâh* (Life). And put thy trust in Him Who lives and dies not; and
    celebrate His praise; and enough is He to be acquainted with the faults
    or His servants. (Quran 25: 58)
11. *Sama'* (Hearing). And God is One who hears and knows (all things).
    (Quran: 24: 21, 60)
12. *Basar* (Sight). And God sees well all that they do. (Quran 3: 163, 5: 71)
13. *Kalâm* (Speaking). And to Moses God spoke direct, (Quran 4: 164)
14. *Qâdir* (Power). In the Judgment of value. (Quran 2: 259, 4: 149).
15. *Murîd* (Fulfilleth His plan). (Quran 11: 253, 11: 108, 4: 164).
16. *'Âlim* (Well-acquainted and has knowledge of all things). (Quran 2: 282,
    9: 115)
17. *Hâyy* (The living). (Quran 2: 255)
18. *Samî'* (Hears). (Quran 24: 21)
19. *Basîr* (Sees). (Quran 3: 163, 4: 74)
20. *Mutakallim* (Spoke direct). (Quran 4: 164).

The author of this book, the *Sifat Dua Puluh,* uses only Quranic verses
as evidence *(dalil)* to support the attributes of God.

The Kitab Jawi and the Role of the Patani Printing Press

The Old (Malay: Kitab Kuning) and New Product

Most of the Kitab Jawi of the leading ulama of Patani were first printed either in Mecca or in Cairo, Egypt, not to mention those that were lithographed during the earlier times in Bombay or published in Constantinople. For the second stage of their history that printing is gradually moved to the printing press of Sulayman Mar'i in Singapore. At the third stage, printing is moved again, this time to Maktabat wa-Matba'at Dar al-Maarif, Penang, Malaysia. Here, the major religious books written by the ulama of Patani are continuously reprinted by the Dar al-Maarif and distributed in Malaysia and Thailand.

These major books of the Patani ulama and some other religious books seem to be stocked in the three Muslim bookstores in the downtown area of Patani: the stores of Muhammad Nahdi, Rudee Road; Haris Trading, Rudee Road; and Kedai Kitab Qayyum, Patani Pirom Road. From these places, Islamic religious books are distributed to every part of the Muslim community in Thailand. These three major bookstores not only distribute the Kitab Jawi but also supply the major Arabic books on *fiqh, tafsîr, nahw, balâghah,* and *tasawwuf*, as well as the Arabic books prepared by some Middle Eastern countries for the madrasah system. Thus, the students of the madrasah system and those of the pondok, as well as other seekers of knowledge, come to buy the necessary books from these bookstores. The two bookstores; Muhammad Nahdi and Haris Trading, observing the customers and the students come to buy the Arabic and religious books during the weekdays. Among the customers are those from Kelantan and Trengganu, the two coastal states of north east Malaysia.

Haris trading is operated by Aslam Haris, a Thai citizen born in Hadramawt. He is helped by his nephew, Muhamad Haris, a Thai citizen born in Indonesia. In an interview with the owner, it was learned that the first distributors of religious Arabic and Jawi books were Haji Abd al-Rashîd Raden Ahmad Jambu and Muhammad Idris Afghan. Aslam Haris told that when he came to Patani in the year 1938 he found only the two distributors mentioned above (interview August 1986). He opened his bookstore in the year 1939 distributing religious books to pondok in various parts of Patani and the areas nearby. He continues in the same work up to the present day. Aslam Haris confirms that the Jawi and Arabic books have become the best sellers, demand for which is increasing every year. This indicates that the need of the people for Jawi and Arabic books has not yet shown any signs of decreasing in spite of the growing strength of the modern system of madrasah, coming into existence to replace the traditional learning system.

This traditional system of teaching, Aslam Haris added, is still being offered, usually in the evenings (Malay: pada waktu malam). According to his observations in the thirties, Aslam Haris says, the students continuously came to study in Pondok Semla, Mango, Dalo and Bermin, as well as Pondok Haji Abd al-Aziz Naprado. Pondok Bermin and Pondok Naprado, Aslam Hâris continues, have really reached the peak of their fame, to the extent that the former has become the center of traditional learning, receiving the Muslims from Bangkok and from other Thai-speaking areas, while the latter, besides being an Islamic center for the Muslims in Thailand, has also become the center of learning for the Indonesian students in more recent times.

Talking with Muhammad Nahdi, the owner of Muhammad Nahdi Bookstore, also a Thai citizen of Hadramawti birth, one may determine that he is also the owner of the printing press Maktabat wa-Matba'at Dar al-Ma arif in Penang, Malaysia. Muhammad Nahdi, 'Amm Nahdi, (Uncle Nahdi) told about his life and how he started his business. When he first came to Patani in the year 1938, he found that there were as Aslam Haris had said, two Muslim bookstores, one of which belonged to Haji Abd al-Rashid Jambu (Raden Ahmad), the owner of Patani Press (Interview September 1988). The other one belonged to Muhammad Idris Afghan, the father of Mr. Qayyum, who at the present time is the owner of the Kedai Kitab Qayyum, Pirom Road, Patani. 'Amm Nahdi opened his bookstore in Patani in the year 1948. On March 4, 1954 he established the printing press in Penang, Malaysia not long after the Sulaymân Mar'i Press in Singapore ceased to function. He had Aslam Haris as his partner in business. By that time (the late, 1940) 'Amm Nahdi had started publishing the Kitab Jawi of the leading ulama of Patani and others in Arabic and Jawi. In 1978, he bought a new, modern printing press and located it at 679/6-7 Soi Surao, Israphap Road, Hiranruji Thonburi, Bangkok 10600, Thailand. This modern press, which carries the name Maktabat wa-Matba'at Muhammad al-Nahdi wa-Awladuhu (Nahdi Press Ltd. Part), is run by his son, Fayiz A. Nahdi who obtained an M.A. degree in Political Science from Karachi University, Pakistan. 'Amm Nahdi told that the new press prints many Arabic books and hundreds of thousands of copies of the Quran ordered by the Kingdom of Saudi Arabia and Kuwait. Among other major Arabic materials coming out of the new press, 'Amm Nahdi says, there are the twenty-five volumes of *al-Mawsû'ah al-Fiqhîyah* (Encyclopedia of Jurisprudence) of the Ministry of Awqaf, Kuwait. These printed volumes are sent back to Kuwait on the instructions of the Awqaf. A large portion of the printed copies of the Quran, according to 'Amm Nahdi, are usually sent to Africa, Pakistan, India, the Philippines and China, as well as being distributed to Malaysia and Thailand.

Local Patani Muslims' Roles in Printing

In the downtown area of Patani itself, there are three Malay-owned printing presses, two of which serve as both bookstores and printing houses. The Saudara Press, Rudee Road (Thai: Mittraphap), belongs to Khâlid Shaykh Salim al-Halabi. During an interview, Khâlid, whose father originally came from Hadramawt, gave the information that the Saudara Press serves only to print the minor works of *kitab kuning* (the old classical Jawi-religious books) written by the Muslims of Patani.

The Patani Press, the other local printed and seller of books, whose owner is Nik Abd. al-Rashid bin Idris Sulayman, a local Malay Muslim publishes some of the major works of Shaykh Ahmad bin Muhammad Zayn bin Mustafa al-Fatani and many other books of the present religious teachers of Patani. These works are produced mainly for the beginners and the common folk of the Malay Muslims in Patani. This Patani Press, 152 Rudee Road, Udom Vithee, in fact produces and distributes mostly Jawi Islamic books.

The third local Malay-owned printing press, whose owner is Mahmud Sa'âd, is the Taman Pustaka Press, Kelapa Road. The printing press, does not serve as a bookstore but produces the works of the present generation of religious teachers of Patani.

These Malay-owned printing presses of Patani play a major role in the proliferation and distribution of Jawi Islamic literature and Arabic textbooks. Through them, the classics of Malay religious literature continue to flourish, fulfilling their vital role. The survival of the Kitab Jawi maintains an important continuity in the tradition of Islamic learning in Patani. These printing presses, indeed, are fundamental to the survival of the Muslim community, in Patani in particular and Thailand as a whole.

CHAPTER 5

The Pondok and the Process of Change

The typical Muslim community in any part of the world will generally seek to follow the same Islamic concept as to how to teach Islam to the children. The differences occur in the way each community implements these educational concepts. The names of Islamic institutions such as *langgar*, madrasah, pondok *pesantren* and pondok can be found easily in Indonesia (Cortes 1984). Some of these names can be found also in the Muslim Philippines. Similarly, in Malaysia, terms such as pondok and madrasah are well-known to the broad spectrum community. Among these institutions the pondok has been a well-respected one in the Malay world perhaps from as far back as the eleventh century until today. In Thailand, especially in the five southern border provinces (Patani, Yala, Narathiwat, Satun and Songkla), the pondok has been known as such to the community for a long time. However, the Islamic education available in the institutions of Patani may have a different approach from that of Indonesia, the Philippines and Malaysia.

Traditionally speaking, the child of any Muslim family starts to learn the Quran at the home of a religious teacher or at the *masjid*. The typical example would be the great modernist, Shaykh Muhammad Abduh of Egypt, who started learning the Quran under his father. Then he was sent to the type of Quranic school known as *kuttâb*. After that, he was sent to the home of hafiz, or professional reciter of the Quran, that he might learn to recite the Quran from memory (Adams 1963). Muslim children in Southeast Asia experience a very similar type of educational process.

In Philippino Muslim communities, the teaching of the Quran occurs in the mosques or in the homes of the *penditas,* (who are also called *gurus*) which is the Sanskrit word for teacher. In Indonesia, the Islamic teaching (called *pengajian*) is conducted in the local prayer houses, which are called *langgar*. Traditionally "seated on the floor around the teacher," as Rosario M. Cortes writes, both beginners and advanced pupils recited the Quranic verses in the chanting tone (Cortes 1984). In fact, they have studied religion and related subjects in the traditional Muslim schools, first the village Quran school, later on the *pesantren* or religious boarding school (Van Nieuwenhuijze 1957). In southern Thailand, in terms of religious teaching, especially in Patani and the areas nearby, the traditional learning environments and methods are still preserved as they were in the past.

As a matter of fact, the religious educational system directed by the religious leaders in the Southeast Asian Islamic areas maintains many of the same features. This can be seen through a comparison of Kelantan and Patani. In the Muslim community in Thailand as a whole and in Patani in particular, the well-known center of religious training where the children sit together daily is called the surau or balaisah, a small prayer house. Both types of learning centers are commonly found in Patani as well as in nearby areas. In these centers, the children learn together how to read the Quran and learn other obligatory precepts known as *fard al-'ayn*.

Before transferring to continue my own education in the Pondok Padang Langa, Chana, in Songkla Province, I used to study in such a place together with other children of my age, but under my parents' and my grandmother's instruction. It is undeniable that participation in such an institution at a very young age has a great influence upon the memory of children thus involved. It is the duty of Muslims, the parents as well as the community, to pave the way to a basic Islamic education for their children.

There are certain major local groups involving themselves in enlightening the Muslim community of Patani, especially in paving the way for young Muslims to receive a basic Islamic education. Wan Kadir bin Che Man classifies the religious elites of Patani society into three groups. The first group is the members of the provincial council for Islamic affairs. The second group is the members of council for the local mosque and the third group comprises religious teachers. According to Che Man, the most influential religious elites are the religious teachers at Islamic schools (pondok), mosques and balaisah in the community (Che Man 1983).

Muslims in the southern border provinces, both Thai and Malay-speaking, are of a close-and-well-knit community with much activity revolving around the mosques and the pondok. Teachers who have a background in Islamic intellectual disciplines, through professionals only in other fields, are respected by society as learned men in those Islamic subjects, but as might be expected, those whose professional training is in Islamic studies have a higher prestige in the Muslim community. This is particularly true in the case of traditional religious teachers (guru). Moreover, they are viewed as the religious figures who most clearly embody the virtues, wisdom and power of Islam in their learning and have a modest and devout personal life styles. In some cases, guru have the popular reputation of being *berkat* or blessed (Winzeler 1985). These teachers are the spiritual guides of the Muslim society in which they reside and the society therefore has a vested interest in ensuring that these people are happy and do not leave them. If they cannot frequently participate in the community through teaching and religious instruction, then the Muslim community wants them to make a visit whenever possible, so that the society can discuss religious matters and learn what is right and what is wrong, according to Islamic precepts. Because of this need, the religious teachers are the most respected people in any Muslim community. This is certainly true for Patani as well as for the substantial Muslim communities in nearby areas such as Songkla, Patthalung, Nakorn Si Thammaraj, Trang, Krabi, Pangnga and Phuket. Surin Pitsuwan observes that those:

Learned individuals, known as the *to'khru* in vernacular, assume the responsibility of instructing and purifying the belief and practice of Islam as their social obligation (fardu kifâya), above and beyond their personal obligation to observe the Islamic precepts (fardu 'ain). They offer religious guidance and spiritual inspiration for individuals and the wider community in their struggle for the fulfillment of the religious duties.

(Pitsuwan 1982).

Thus, the society must preserve an Islamic education process that begins with the Quranic school (kuttâb) and promote the traditional intellectual institutions that follow.

Traditional and Modern Teachers

What is meant by the 'traditional' teachers here is that they are the *tok gurus*. These teachers have usually trained in the traditional institutions, first in Patani and then perhaps in the *Masjid* al-Haram in Mecca, in the *Masjid* al-Nabawi in Medina and the *Masjid* al-Azhar in Cairo, Egypt. These teachers are usually trained under certain specialized *shaykhs* (learned scholars in Islam) and have become the qualified professional masters of certain subjects in particular fields. They have no degrees in the modern sense. However, they are usually given certain certificates, called *ijazah* in the centuries-old system of Islamic learning. The qualified student, Ibn Khaldun explains, may have obtained the approval of the *shaykh* for transmitting (*munawalah*) written material in his name, or he may have obtained his permission (*ijazah*) to transmit certain traditions (hadith) (Ibn Khaldun 1958).

The modern teachers are those who went through modern formal institutions of learning in Thailand and Muslim countries, and obtained the degrees now usually conferred, the B.A., M.A. or Ph. D. These modern teachers are usually called ustaz. After having studies methods of learning and teaching they usually teach in madrasahs. Now, these groups of *ustaz* are very active in providing Arabic and Islamic education to the Muslim children in southern Thailand. They are also highly respected people in the Muslim community.

The Pondok: Its Structure and Daily Routine

The Islamic education in the Muslim community in Thailand starts at the homes of religious teachers, at the balaisah or at the masjid (mosque). Then, for more intensive training at a higher level, the children have to go elsewhere. The parents usually send them to study at certain pondok and hope that they will become the leaders of their own community, or at least know how to take responsibility as good Muslims towards their families.

In medieval Islam, the madrasah was the highest educational institution of Islam and the development of the madrasah, somewhat paralleling in function of the college of modern times, occurred in three stages: from the masjid to the masjid-khan complex, to the madrasah (Makdisi 1981).

Carefully observing the learning process in the pondok of Patani, with special attention to how it relates to the madrasah of medieval Islam and yet without comparing or contrasting the two institutions in any great detail, we find that the intellectual process in both is almost the same. The pondok of Patani, however, preserves its function today and continues to bring education to Muslim communities, though not in as broad a way as did the medieval form of the learning institution. The differing intellectual maturity of the students is the most important factor that makes the learning process different in the two. The differences become clearer when we look at the learning system in the masjid of medieval Islam and that of Patani. This is because the system of the former concentrated deeply on law and its component subjects:

The basic law course of the masjid, usually lasting a period of four years, required a place of residence for the law students who came to it from out-of-town; whence the development of the masjid-khan complex.

(Makdisi 1981)

By contrast, the teaching in the masjid in Patani, as well as in Thailand as a whole, concentrates only on a basic instruction in the reading of the Quran and the practical understanding of the *fard* '*ayn*. This is because most of the children are very young and they tend to be the children of parents engaged in the more manual occupations. There is, however, regular teaching being conducted for largely adult audiences by certain learned people in the masjid on Friday morning.

In Patani, when these children who have attended the masjid classes reach the age of eleven or twelve years and have also finished Thai compulsory public education, some of them are sent to study in pondok and some others, if they do not leave school, might continue in the Thai government schools. Those that must go away from home to study in pondok normally need to have places to reside in for a number of years. Thus, the pondok fulfils the same role as a type of an independent boarding school.

In many cases, parents will build for their children small, comfortable huts commonly known as pondok and thus, the name of the type of institution. These are typically shared by two or three students. These small comfortable huts were, in the past, built of wood and bamboo with palm thatch roof and like most other buildings are set several feet off the ground (Winzeler 1985). Around the pondok area there are the houses of the guru and the guru's assistants. The houses of the couples with families are usually built in a special area called *pondok dalae* (inner lodging hut) in the Patani Malay dialect. This will also be the area which is devoted to housing for the female students and the married couples. The huts of the male students are located in a separate area called the *pondok luar* (Malay, "outer lodging hut" with the runround). The terms pondok dalae and pondok luar are called by the Thai-speaking Muslims *ponok nai* and *ponok nok*. The houses that are built in the pondok dalae generally seem to be more permanent than those in the pondok luar. This is because the huts that are built in the male students' area are temporarily constructed, due to the unknown duration and temporary stay of the male students while seeking knowledge.

One has to understand that the daily life of the pondok starts very early in the morning, before dawn. The students have to wake up before the Fajr al-Sâdiq (true dawn) during which the time of dawn prayer, Solat al-Fajr, starts. Usually, the first *âdhân* calling for prayer is made prior to the true dawn, so that the students will have enough time to bath and perform the ablutions (*wudû'*). In some pondok, the *tok guru*s go to each student's lodging hut and awake them by calling out "solat, solat" (prayer, prayer!). Always heard in the Âdhân of the dawn prayer is the phrase: "*Al-Salâh tu khayr min al-naum*" ("Prayer is better than sleep"). At this particular moment, nobody should still be sleeping, but should already be joining the lines (*sufûf*, pl. of *saff*) of the Solat al-Fajr with fellow students. Before worship begins, the tok guru might go to the students' lodging once again to check whether any remain sleeping.

The balaisah (called *balay* by the Thai-speaking Muslims) is full of students lining up to perform the Solat al-Fajr. After the Solat al-fajr the *tok guru*, sitting on the floor, turns towards the *anak-anak murid* (students) and reads aloud from the books that are being studied; a reading which may be in either Arabic or Jawi. This depends on how well-versed the guru is. If the text is in Arabic, the interpretation or explanation is made in Malay (usually in the Patani Malay dialect).

Questions are also put to the students throughout the instruction. The junior and the senior students may sit in the front rows and they are usually asked certain questions that might remind them of the linguistic structures involved in the reading. Question might be repeatedly asked by the tok guru, calling upon certains students by name, from whom the correct detailed responses are expected. Questions are asked while teaching not only to know how far the students understand the texts and how closely they are paying attention to them, but also, to observe how well the students are prepared and how well they are acquinted with other subjects that lead them to understand the texts. That is to say, they are required to know subjects like *nahw* (grammer), *sarf* (morphology) and *balâghah* (rhetoric).

Traditionally the teachers had to discuss the different subjects taught, hear criticism offered and answer and satisfy the students on all points raised by them (Shushtery 1938).

The traditional intellectual learning method in fact, has "no system of education nor fixed syllabus, each professor (tok guru) is having his own method of teaching and syllabus" (Shustery 1938). The popular Arabic books that are used as texts and read in the pondok of Patani, even today besides the Kitab Jawi, are as follows:

1. Nahw and Sarf (Grammar and Morphology)

a. Kitab *Shadh al-'Uraf fî Fann al-Sarf* by Ahmad al-Hamlâwî (1932).
b. *Sharh Ibn 'Aqîl 'alá' al-Alfiyah* by Ibn Malik (1274).
c. *Hâshîyah 'alá' Sharh al-Fâkihî li-Qatr al-Nadá* by Yasin ibn Zayn al-Din.
d. *Tashwîq al-Khullân 'alâ' Sharh al Ajurrûmîyah* by Sayyid Ahmad Zayni Dahlan (1816 or 7 - 1886).
e. *al-Sujâ'î 'alá' al-Qatr* by Ibn al-Hisham.
f. *Matn al-Ajurrûmîyah* bt Abu Abd Allah Muhammad ibn Dawud al-Sinhaji known as Ibn Ajurrûm (1273 or 4-1323).
g. *Matn al-Binâ wa-al-Asâs* by 'Allâmah Mullâ 'Abd Allâh al-Danaqzî.

2. Fiqh (Islamic Jurisprudence)

a. *Qalyûbî wa-'Umâyrah* by Shihâb al-Dîn al-Qalyûbî and Shaykh 'Umayrah.
b. *Fath al-Wahhâb bi-Sharh Manhaj al-Tullâb* by Shaykh al-Islam Abi Yahya Zakariya al-Ansari (1413 - 1520).
c. *Mughnî al-Muhtâj ilâ Ma'rifat Alfâz al-Minhâj* of al-Shaykh Muhammad al-Shirbini al-Khatib (1570).
d. *al-Hashîyah* of al-Shaykh 'Abd Allâh ibn Hijâzî ibn Ibrahim al-Shafi'i al-Azhari al-Shahir bi-al-Sharqawi (1737 or 8 - 1812).
e. *Hâsyîyah al-Bayyûmi 'alá' al-Manhaj* by Sulaiman ibn Umar bin Muhammad al-Bujayri al-Shafii
f. *al-Ashbâh wa-al-Nazâ'ir fî-Qawâ'id wa-Furû' Fiqh al-Shâfi'î* by al-Imâm Jalal al-Din Abd al-Rahman ibn Ab Bakr al-Suyuti (1445 - 1505).
g. *al-Hâshîyah 'alâ Sharh Umm al-Barâhîn* by Muhammad ibn al-Dasûqî.
h. *al-Iqnâ' fi Hall Alfâz Abî Shujâ* by Shaykh Muhammad Shirbini al-Khatib (1570).

3.Tafsir (Quran commentary)

a. al-Futûhât al-Ilâhîyah by Sulayman ibn Umar al-'Ujaylî al-Shafi'i al Shahîr bi-al-Jamal.

b. Tafsîr al-Jalâlayn by Jalal al-Din Abd Rahman ibn Abi Bakr al-Suyuti (1445 - 1505) and Jalal al-Din Muhammad ibn Ahmad al-Mahalli (1389-1459).

4. Hadith (Prophetic tradition)

a. al-Adhkâr Muntakhaba min Kalâm Sayyid al-Abrâr by al-Imam Muhyi al-Din Abî Zakariya Yahya ibn Sharaf al-Nawawi al-Dimishqî al-Shâfi'î.

b. Riyâd al-Salihin min Kalâm Sayyid al-Mursalîn by al-Imam al-Muhaddith al-Hafiz Muhyî al-Dîn Abî Zakarîyâ Yahyâ ibn Sharaf al-Nawawi (1233 - 1277).

c. Subul al-Salâm by al-Imam Muhammad ibn Ismail al-Kahlânî

d. Bulûgh al-Murâm by al-Hafiz Shihâb al-Dîn Abî al-Fald Ahmad ibn Muhammad ibn Hajar al-'Asqalânî (1372 - 1449).

e. Jawâhir al-Bukhârî wa-Sharh al-Qastallânî by Mustafá Muhammad 'Imârah.

f. Matn al-Bukhârî by Abu Abd Allah ibn Ismail al-Bukhari (810-870).

g. Sunan Abî Dâwûd by al-Imam Abi Dawud Sulayman (817 or 8-889).

5. Balâghah (Rhetoric)

a. al-Jawâhir al-Maknûn fi-al-Ma'âni wa-al Bayân wa-al-Badî by Shaykh Ahmad Damanhûrî.

The above are some of the Arabic books that are being used to educate the students in the pondok. These books are available in either Nahdi Bookstore or Haris Trading in the town of Patani. The tok guru utilize these books and others, depending on their own personal choice.

These then, are the feature of the pondok situated in the Malay-speaking community. The situation may be slighty different in those pondok that are located among the Thai-speaking Muslims. The teaching there is also conducted through either Arabic or Jawi texts. In the pondok where the majority speaks Thai, the texts are translated into the local Thai dialect through Malay, if the texts are in Arabic. The Malay language, at this point, still plays an important role as a medium of achieving understanding of the full texts. Not only that, but the Malay language also allows the student to understand the grammatical structures involved in the Arabic texts.

For example, when an Arabic word sentence like *Arkân al-Islam khamsah,* (The pillars of Islam are five) is translated into Melayu, we find that the first part of this sentence (*Arkân al-Islam,*) would be translated as *Bermula rukun*

Islam itu, and the second part (*khamsah*, would be translated *ialah lima perkara*. The noun in the first part of this sentence, that is *rukun* (Malay spelling) (Ar., arkân) would grammatically identified as the *mubtada* (Ar., subject). This grammatical term is indicated by the Malay word *bermula*. So, in understanding the Arabic grammar, whenever the Malay translation begins with *bermula,* the student will be taught that the noun that comes immediately after it is the *mubtada'* (Ar., subject). The Malay translation of the second part of the sentence starts with either *iaitu* or *ialah*. It indicates that the noun that comes immediately after it is the *khabar* (Ar., predicate). So, the whole translation for the sentence, *Arkân al-Islam khamsah,* runs: *Bermula rukun Islam itu iaitu (ialah) lima perkara.* Similarly, other Malay morphological and grammatical labels are incorporated into the translation to help the students understand the structure of the original Arabic text. Zamakhsyari Dhofier explains that:

> The translation is given word by word and in such a way that the student will know not only the meaning of the words, but also the position of the words in the sentences. Thus the student learns the Arabic grammar directly from particular passages.
>
> (Dhofier 1978)

However, it is worth noting here that the Malay used in this traditional grammatical analyses and translations is the classical Malay language and not the contemporary language. These methods are universally practiced in the pondok, especially with the novice students. Thus, we realize that the Kitab Jawi and the Malay language are of fundamental importance in the traditional method of learning Arabic texts.

Morning Session

The daily routine of the intellectual learning process in the pondok is normally divided into three sessions. First, it is the morning session. This session covers at least two hours, during which the teacher may read two kitabs. This session starts immediately after Solat al-Subh (Dawn Prayer). After the morning lesson, the students will go back to their rooms and cook their morning meal. Some take their breakfast at the small coffee house nearby which often also doubles as the grocery. During the rest period, the beginners as well as the elementary students may go to read specific kitab under the tok guru's helpers, known as *ketua muṯâla'ah* in Malay or *hua na muṯola'ah* in Thai. These assistants are very helpful in reviewing what has been taught by the tok guru. The beginners usually study with one or another of these assistants in any subjects that they are persuing under the tok guru. The assistants are qualified to give instructions in particular subjects. The beginners know what subject they need to review and to which assistant they should go to do their reviewing (*muṯâla'ah*: Arabic) or under whom they want to practice.

During my field research in August and September of 1986 and in the same months of 1987, I had the good fortune to meet several religious teachers of both traditional and modern systems of teaching in Patani together with their assistants, most of whom are their sons-in-law. I also met a number of the sons of these tok guru who are the graduates of the Middle Eastern universities. Most of the tok guru sons-in-law are products of the pondok system. In other words, they are the former students of the pondok and have never studied outside their walls. Among the best examples would be the following sons-in-law of tok guru:

1. Tok Guru Abd al-Rahman Adam, originally from Prathum Thani Province, one of the central provinces of Thailand, is the son-in-law of Tok Guru Bermin, Haji Ahmad Idris. At the present time, this Tok Guru, Abd al-Rahman Adam, is taking full responsibility for teaching at the pondok, since the death of his father-in-law. During his father-in-law's lifetime, he used to teach for him as an assistant. Tok Guru Abd al-Rahman Adam is now known as Tok Guru Bermin. He still serves the Muslim students through the traditional teaching methods, though the modern type of madrasah instruction has also been brought into his school. The madrasah system has been brought in due to the need of the beginners who have no background in Arabic, Islamic subjects, or Malay. In his pondok, several junior and senior students help him in the teaching process in both traditional and modern system.

    It is worth mentioning here that there is no Thai educational program in this pondok, even though the Thai authorities have urged him to incorporate the Thai education curriculum into that of his pondok. Tok Guru Abd al-Rahman Adam has not accepted the government's program, not because Thai education is not important, but because he wants Islamic learning to be free from government control. He also believes that the students who come to study at his pondok do not need more than the years of compulsory Thai education which they have already received. What they really need at their point of entry is an Islamic education. In fact, the students who come to study in any pondok in Patani have already finished their Thai compulsory education. If they really needed to study Thai at a higher level, Tok Guru Abd al-Rahman Adam said, they should go to the Thai schools that provide Thai education throughout the country (Interview 1986). So, his pondok remains purely a center for Islamic learning, attracting its students from all parts of the country, both Thai and Malay-speaking groups.

2. Tok Guru Haji Husayn Dalo is son-in-law of the late Haji Abd al-Rahman Arshadi, known as Tok Guru Dalo, whose son is Tok Guru Haji Muhammad commonly known as Khali. Khali also taught for a number of years at his father's pondok. Khali died in 1987, a little less than a

year after I met him during my first research visit between August and September 1986. His brother in-law, Haji Husayn, who used to be an assistant, is now in full charge of his own pondok next to his father in-law's place. His fame in the traditional system of learning has drawn a large number of students from throughout the country. Known as Tok Guru Dalo, like his late father-in-law, Haji Husayn has taken a firm stance in providing an ideal Islamic education. Indeed, it would be fair to record that the reputation of the Pondok Dalo continues to link its present message to its past glory.

3. Haji 'Abd Allah is the son-in-law of Tok Guru Haji Ahmad Perigi, Patani. Haji Ahmad is now 107 years of age; and is still active in his teaching. Haji Abd Allah spent fifteen years studying under his father-in-law. He also studied under Tok Guru Dalo, the late Haji Abd al-Rahman Arshadi. Before coming back to teach at Pondok Perigi, he spent thirteen years studying in Masjid al-Haram, Mecca (Interview Sept. 11, 1987). As a son-in-law and having trained in the traditional way, Haji 'Abd Allah is responsible for teaching the major books that deal with *fiqh, usûl al-fiqh*, tafsir, Hadith, *nahw* and *sarf*. His activities run side-by-side with his father-in-law's. This traditional way of learning and teaching was also shared by Yahya, the son of Tok Guru Haji Ahmad Perigi. Yahya, who spent all of his youth studying under his father and has never been abroad, told me that he started teaching the students when he felt competent in the subjects learned from his father (Interview 11 Sept. 1987).

In this pondok, the madrasah system has been introduced and it is run by the son of the tok guru, Ustâdh Ramlî and his wife Ustazah Hasnah. Both are graduates from a Middle Eastern university. As a young graduate, Ustaz Ramli is trying very hard to gear the madrasah system up to the level recognized by Muslim countries. His wife, Ustazah Hasnah, takes the roles of a mother and a mentor in providing Islamic education for preschool children in a type of kindergarten organized under her supervision. This type of kindergarten is considered to be the first private project of its kind ever established in a village of Patani by graduates from Middle Eastern universities.

4. Haji Qasem bin Haji Dawud, and Haji Abd Allah bin Abd al-Rahman are the assistants of Pondok Baba Yeh, Tok Jong, Nongchik, Patani. Both are the sons-in-law of Haji Idris bin Haji Wan Ali Bakum, known as Baba Yeh. These two young assistants, not yet thirty, are responsible for teaching most of the major religious and Arabic books to the students in the pondok. Both Haji Qasem and Haji Abd Allah have never studied Islam or the Arabic language abroad.

Haji Qasem, a native of Kampung Bangrai, a Malay-speaking village about two miles from the pondok where he is now teaching and raising his family, told that while he was attending Thai public schools in his village, he started studying Islam at a *tadika* school (a sort of Islamic kindergarten) and then went to study under Haji Hamzah, the Tok Guru of Pondok Hutan Agu, in the Nongchik area. At the time of this interview, Haji Qasem was twenty-six years of age and in his eleventh year of study in the pondok under Baba Yeh. At the same time, he was serving his fellow students as the tok guru's helper together with his other friends and senior students (Interview 26 August, 1987).

Haji Abd Allah bin Abd al-Rahman is originally from Ban Plee, a Thai-speaking area of the Nathawee District, Songkla Province. He came to study under Baba Yeh fifteen years ago and now he is teaching the major Islamic and Arabic books hand-in-hand with the tok guru and with his other helpers. He serves both those students whose mother tongue is Thai and those who speak Malay. As young as any one could imagine, yet taking such a highly respected position with maturity, Haji Abd Allah bin Abd al-Rahman holds the high esteem of his fellow students and the community at large (Interview 26 Sept. 1986).

The assistants to tok guru must have an authorization from the tok guru themselves, so that they can be regarded as being fully able to transmit the knowledge they learn from their respective tok guru to the beginners. These assistants, after being considered qualified in certain subjects, are given an ijazah, the traditional certificate of authorization, normally accompanied by and couched in characteristic spoken phrases such as: *Aku idhinkan engkau mengajar* kitab *fiqah/tafsir dengan berkat Allah subhânahu wa-ta'âlâ.* Which literally means "I confer on you permission to teach the book of *fiqh/tafsîr* with the blessing of Allah (Interview 5 Sept. 1987). To confirm these statements, Fazlur Rahman writes:

The teacher, after giving his full course, personally gave a certificate (ijazah) to the student who was then allowed to teach. The certificate was sometimes given in an individual subject -- say *fiqh* or Hadîth. Sometimes it concerned several subjects and sometimes it was valid only for specified books which the pupil had read.

(Rahman 1987)

Afternoon Session and Evening Session

The second session of the learning process in pondok is the afternoon session. This session is usually conducted after Solat al-Zuhr (noon prayer). This session may continue up to the time of Solat al-'Asr (the afternoon prayer). The break period starts after the Solat al-Asr. The third and the last session of the day starts immediately after Solat al-Maghrib (the prayer after sunset), and continues until the Solat al-'Isyak' (the night prayer). This is the traditional routine of pondok life in Patani and the areas nearby.

During the evening, some students and the juniors and seniors always stay up late at night reviewing the subjects and memorizing what they have jotted down during the long day. Anyone passing by the pondok (student's lodging hut) during the quiet hours of late evening may hear chanting tones or the sound of oral practice, indicating the learning by rote of some *matn* (text). Rote learning and jotting down the commentary in the margins or beneath the texts are important features of traditional Muslim learning. "The development of the memory is a constant feature of medieval education in Islam" (Makdisi 1981). Once again Makdisi's work is refered to which shows the universality of traditional Islamic learning, even in the pondok system of Patani:

Commiting materials to writing was recognized as most important in the process of learning. Memory alone was not to be trusted. Recording was also to be done from the 'mouths of the professors' and from their works, and when the work was considered important, it was copied whole. Muhammad b. Muslim b. Wara (265/879), upon his arrival in Baghdad from Cairo, went to pay a visit to Ahmad b. Hanbal who asked him. 'Did you copy the books of Shafi'i?' Ibn Wara answered, 'No'. Where upon Ibn Hanbal admonished him, saying: 'You were remiss. We did not come to know the difference between the general ('umum) and the particular (khusus) statements in scripture, nor between abrogating (nasikh) and abrogated (mansukh) hadîths until we had attended the lessons (and taken down the dictation) of Shafi'i. Upon hearing this, Ibn Wara turned back to Cairo and copied the works of Shafi'i.

(Makdisi 1981)

Thus, the methodology of pondok education in southern Thailand was and is, to some degree, similar to the widely recognized system of the intellectual learning process among the institutions in medieval Islam. We also see that most of the subjects taught in the pondok correspond to what has been taught throughout the history of Islamic institutions. The subjects of *fiqh* (jurisprudence), *uṣûl al-fiqh* (principles of jurisprudence), hadith (Prophetic tradition), tafsir (Quran commentary) and *kalâm* (theology) are taught in most Muslim institutions and are being taught in the pondok of Patani. In addition, subjects like *akhlâq* (ethics), *tasawwuf* (ṣufism), *naḥw* (Arabic grammar) *ṣarf* (morphology), *balâghah* (rhetoric), *farâ'id* (division of inheritance) and *manṭiq* (logic) are also offered in the pondok (Rahman 1987; Dodge 1962).

However, not all pondok have the same specializations. Some may specialize in *naḥw* and the teacher is then known as "Tok Nahu" (a Malay expression, Arabic: Ahl al-Naḥw). Another may specialize in *fiqh* and the teacher is called "Tok Faqih" (a Malay expression, Arabic: al-Faqîh). Because of these differences, students normally move from one *pondok* to another in order to gain more knowledge across a range of different fields. Throughout the year, the phenomenon of students transferring from one place to another can be seen. In the course of seeking knowledge *(talab al-'ilm)*, students move from one place to another depending on the subject they want to specialize in. The changing of places (Malay: *pindah tempat*) regularly occurs among the junior and senior students. Here Fazlur Rahman notes that students travelled over long distances, sometimes, over the length and breadth of the Muslim world to follow the lectures of famous teachers (Rahman 1987). Moreover, we learn that in those days, not only the students but also scholars used to travel and take long journeys in search of knowledge. Sometimes, an Iranian went as far as Spain and other times a Spanish scholar was found studying in the extreme East (Shushtery 1938).

At the southern Malay Muslim identity level, the pondok or traditional system in Patani has produced several very competent tok gurus or local ulama in certain fields. Among those whose names have been mentioned by Islamic scholars and whose works have been read and referred to as major sources for understanding Islam by the Muslims of the Malay world are the great four leading figures earlier mentioned.

The Pondok: Present and Future

That pondok have survived can be traced back to two important factors: the continuation of teaching in the traditional way with the traditional texts and the means of financial support. In the teaching process, the *pondok* depends directly upon the reputation of the tok guru himself. His specialization in a certain field, as well as his personality, can easily draw the attention of students to study with him. The more the students come to study at his pondok the more financial support the tok guru receives from the community. The pondok generally cannot stand on its own feet, but relies partly or wholly upon the financial support provided by the community because it has no independent income, not even tuition fees. It depends solely upon zakat (alms, donations, or charity) and is more or less like other Muslim institutions that were based on the law of 'Waqf' or charitable trust (Makdisi 1981). Through donations, the tok guru earn their living. Through charitable trusts, the pondok can earn income from several acres of a rubber plantation, coconut trees, or other income-producing property. The zakat (charity tax of a padi field owned by a supporter) may be given regularly once a year after the harvest. This is the financial system that keeps the pondok alive.

Another factor, no less important than the financial support, is the continuity of teaching through a succession of generations. The tok guru prepares his son-in-law or another young tok guru for the day when he will succeed him. This son-in-law takes over in time and runs the pondok, trying to follow in the footsteps of the old tok guru. He is usually known already in the community because he has taught side-by-side with the tok guru. Thus, the Muslims in the area know him and expect him to become the tok guru*'s* successor. In some pondok, though not many, the son of the tok guru, takes on this responsibility after his father's death. However, in most cases:

A son-in-law who becomes a teacher in the pondok keeps it going after the guru's death but for the most part this is a matter of the new guru having begun over again to acquire of following and develop a reputation rather than one of succeeding to an established position within the wider community.

(Winzeler 1985)

The Pondok and the Process of Adaptation

After the Second World War, a number of progressive Muslims of Patani began to consider developing the pondok, a loose and unstructured system, into a more systematic method of instruction so as to cope with the demands proposed by the Thai government. Thus, the pondok institution was gradually changed into an Islamic private school system comprising 122 pondoks. This is the number of pondok which were officially registered with the government in 1961/2504 B.E., the beginning of the pondok registration program. By the final year of registration, 1971/2514 B.E., more than four hundred pondoks had accepted the government program of registration. This included the pondoks in regions Two, Three and Four (Karnpim 1986). Region Two includes Patani, Yala, Narathiwat and Satun, whereas Songkla, Nakorn Si Thammaraj and Patthalung are in Region Three, and Phuket, Pangnga, Krabi and Ranong, as well as Trang, are in Region Four (Office of P.E.C. 1986).

The process of institutional change has made the Muslim people aware of the coming of the modern trends into their traditional institutions. To speak of 'modern trends' makes Muslim religious leaders wonder what is going to happen if such terms carry the meaning they seem to. Besides not being well-prepared in modern fields of education, traditional Muslims also know that Islamic education is totally different from what the secularists think an education should be. This is because:

Islamic education does not regard life as an end in itself. Life on earth is but a bridge which man must cross before he enters into spiritual life after death. Herein lies a fundamental difference between modern and Islamic education. Modern education merely considers happiness in his world as its final goal, whereas Islamic education regards life as only a means of achieving happiness in the hereafter. This basic difference in the aims and objectives of modern and Islamic education leads to differences in the methods by which these aims and objectives are achieved ... On the other hand Islamic education sees the happiness of man as fundamentally based on intellectual, emotional and spiritual convictions ... In Islam there is no segregation between religious and secular education. They are inseparable and indivisible. Neither aspect should be over-emphasized at the expense of the other.

(al-Afendi & A. Balach 1980)

In order to face the new challenges of government educational policy, the Muslims of Patani and surrounding areas started to think of how to maintain their traditional Islamic heritage and at the same time adjust to the national policies whose goals were those of an adequate education for modern life and the integration of ethnic groups in the nation. To uphold their Islamic heritage, many parents have been sending their children to study in Muslim countries including those of the Middle East; thus, a further blending of the domestic with the outside world. Under the new storm of the government's socio-economic development effort, the Muslim of Thailand as a whole and of southern Thailand in particular have sent their children to Middle Eastern countries in the hope that they will be properly taught in Arabic and oriented Islam. These responses began in 1960 and continue until today and were encouraged when several Middle Eastern countries began their own educational policies of encouraging and supporting young Muslims to study Arabic and Islam in the Middle East with special financial aid.

In Egypt, during the late President Gamal Abdel Nasser's era and the late President Muhammad Anwar al-Sadat's, scholarships were offered to bring foreign students to al-Azhar University (Fischer 1982). Official Islamic organizations, with names such as "Hay'at al-Awqâf wa-al-Majlis al-A'lâ lil-Shu'ûn al-Islâmîyah" (The Organization of Charitable Trusts and the Supreme Council for Islamic Affairs), of countries like the Kingdom Saudi Arabia, Iraq, Kuwait, Libya, Sudan, Tunisia, Algeria and Egypt are funding most of the Muslim students from Thailand, either through official or private channels, with the type of financial aid known as *al-minhah al-dirâsîyah* (educational scholarship). In some of these countries, the students receive stipends or pocket money in addition to their lodging and food. In Egypt, most of the sponsored male students stay in a dormitory called Madînat al-Bu'ûth al-Islâmîyah (The Islamic Missions City), in Abbasiah, Cairo, while the female students mostly funded by al-Majlis al-A'lâ lil-Shu'ûn al-Islâmîyah, in Garden City, Cairo, stay in Dâr al-Diyâfah al-Islâmîyah (The Islamic Guest House), Dayr al-Malâk, Misr and Sudan Street, Cairo. The number of Thai Muslim students studying in Cairo increases every year. They come to study in various fields, mostly at Al-Azhar University. They are now better prepared for this experience than previous generations. The new system of learning provided by the Islamic private schools or madrasahs certainly nourishes them and provides them with the background and skills to cope with the learning system of al-Azhar and other Middle Eastern institutions (Table 5.1).

The record book of The Thai Students' Association in Cairo provides figures on the totals of students since the establishment of the Association in 1955 (Table 5.1). Most of these students are concentrated in the city of Cairo and studying in al-Azhar University, though a few of them also study at Cairo University, 'Ayn Shams University, Tanta University, Alexandria University of al-Ma'had al-Fannî al-'Âlî, at Shubra. There are even Thai Muslims at the

American University in Cairo. Note that the figures in Table 5.1 show those students beginning their study in Cairo. According to the record book of the Thai Students' Association, the *total* number of students studying in Cairo in the year 1987, was 750 students. Of these, three hundred students had scholarships.

TABLE 5.1 Number of Thai Students studying in Cairo,
Egypt, 1955-87

Year	Number of Students	Year	Number of Students
1955	16	1972	12
1956	6	1973	20
1957	0	1974	43
1958	3	1975	49
1959	5	1976	57
1960	18	1977	61
1961	8	1978	136
1962	25	1979	195
1963	35	1980	84
1964	44	1981	159
1965	1	1982	92
1966	26	1983	95
1967	19	1984	84
1968	8	1985	103
1969	5	1986	35
1970	21	1987	30
1971	16		

The regional distribution is 60% from Southern Thailand, 39% from Central Thailand including Bangkok and 2% from the North. All of these students have Thai academic backgrounds. Thus, 25% of them have earned the high school certificate (Thai: Mathyom suksa 5 or Mathyom 6), 60% have earned the lower school certificate (Thai: Mathyom suksa 3) and 15% have earned the elementary school certificate (Thai: Prathom suksa 7 or 6). Some of them have studied Arabic and religion with 35% have a strong Arabic and religious background, 40% have some, and 25% have no background.

It is remarkable that: in the 19th century, Patani students went almost exclusively to Mecca for study, but towards the end of the century and certainly by the 1920's, they were attending al-Azhar University in Cairo as well (Matheson & Hooker 1988). It is also reported that in 1919, there were about fifty to sixty students studying in Cairo from Indonesia (mostly West Sumatera), with perhaps an additional twenty from Peninsular Malaya and Southern Thailand (Roff 1970).

In Cairo they studied in various schools, depending on the strength of their Arabic background and their general academic knowledge. Though most students from Asia had come to Cairo to further their religious education, one could hardly say that their political education was being neglected (Roff 1970). In Mecca or Cairo, they adjusted themselves to the madrasah system there, studying subjects that qualified them for a higher education.

Those who obtained their higher school certificates in sciences or arts, say from the Kingdom of Saudi Arabia or Egypt, could easily enter the appropriate university degree programs at Cairo University in the Faculty of Commerce, Political Science or even Medical School. It was the student generations of the 1950's that did this. Through the educational development of Thailand, the generations of the 1960's and the 1970's had a better chance of moving directly from Thailand to the higher academic institutions in Cairo; for the latter might be better prepared in their homeland in general educations and perhaps in Arabic and Islamic Studies than they formerly had been. Moreover, some of the graduates of the 50's and 60's after returning home, stepped into the administrative offices of the government and some have become pioneers in government service in the Ministry of Foreign Affairs.

Among the pioneers, are Pisut Hajidin and Ahmad Samadi. Hajidin who is known as Haji Abd al-Rashid Hajidin, is originally from Narathiwat Province whereas Samadi is a Muslim from Bangkok. Both are graduates of Cairo University. The former was a political science student while the latter was a student at Dar al-Ulum. Hajidin served as the representative of Thailand to the United Nations for some years. He later served as a *chargé d'affaires* of the Royal Thai Embassy at Jeddah, and now works in the Protocol Department in the Ministry of Foreign Affairs. Mr. Samadi did not serve long in his diplomatic career. He worked as a staff member of the Royal Thai Embassy in Kuala Lumpur for one term, and then was sent to Jeddah for several years. Since resigning from his diplomatic employment, Mr. Samadi has worked for his own company in Bangkok. Of these two, Pisut Hajidin was a product of the pondok system of education.

The successful involvement of young graduates, like these from the Middle Eastern universities, in the Thai government sectors, working side-by-side with the graduates from the national universities of Thailand, has removed the veil of doubt and the suspicion of inadequacy that has previously clung to the education achieved through the Arabic medium. Thus, the Thai people's negative attitude in general and the Muslims' in particular has gradually vanished.

The Government's Policy for Education in the Four Southern Provinces of Thailand

The Major Policy, the National Identity and Muslims' Attitudes

1. Improving the Pondok and Changing It into an Officially Accepted System

In the year 1970/2513 B.E., the Ministry of Education carried out the policy of improving the Islamic Private Schools under the Improvement Project of the Ministry of Education, 1970. The primary objectives of this policy were to bring the education of the pondok into line with the levels of the national standard of education and to build a better understanding between the government and the people. In the year 1973/2516 B.E., the Prime Minister's Cabinet made this decision by forming the Improvement Committee for the Islamic Private Schools to give advice to the Ministry of Education to help it to reach the stated national education objectives.

The Islamic Private School is a private school as mentioned in the 1982, Act 15 (2) of the Thai legal code. According to the Ministry of Education Act dated November 24, 1982/2525 B.E., it is also a religious school under the supervision and promotion of the office of the Private Education Committee, which is within the Ministry of Education.

Although Islamic private schools can be found throughout Thailand, Region Two or "Khet Karn Suksasong" in Thai, as well as Region Three and Region Four concern this study. These schools developed from the traditional institutions, the pondok, which were built by the tok guru for instructing people to live according to Islamic beliefs. As Islamic private schools, they continue this mission of providing Islamic education but, more and more, they also offer academic and professional courses.

The Ministry of Education has developed the educational process in the four southern provinces in accord with the Educational Development Program used throughout the country. In Region Two, where majority of the people speak Malay, there are traditional institutions scattered everywhere, but they are not necessarily administered in accordance with current government regulation. Thus, the Ministry of Education needed to take the initiative by:

1. Encouraging the pondok to officially register as legally recognized pondok.
2. Encouraging the already registered pondok to transform themselves into Islamic private schools.
3. Not allowing new pondok to be established outside of the regional school system.

The Ministry of Education and the Ministry of Interior had the mandate to intergrate licensed pondok institutions into the regional system within a time scale of three to five years. As a result, there are now 487 registered pondok out of which 426 have become Islamic private schools and sixty-one have ceased to function. The result has been a radical change in Islamic education and the perceptions of it among the southern Muslim people of Thailand.

The policy of the government is to bring the Malay Muslims of the four southern provinces into the full consciousness of having a Thai identity. This is approached through the educational policy by encouraging the pondok to accept the Thai education proposed by the Ministry of Education. Through introducing Thai education into the Islamic private school, the government hopes that the Thai language will take over from the Arabic as well from the Malay languages and there after replace them in their daily lives. The Malay language, which is the mother tongue of the Malay Muslims in these areas, has not faded away as the government might have hoped. Rather, it adapted itself to the situation under the new techniques of modern education which are guided in practise by the young Malay Muslim graduates. In fact, in both pondok and madrasah system, side-by-side with the Arabic language, the Malay language grows in the extent of its use as a result of the influence of young graduates from neighbouring Islamic countries. This corresponds to what Astri Suhrke says: "Ethnic boundaries as symbolised by the centrality of the pondok and the Malay language have not been markedly weakened, despite the government's very considerable investment in Thai public education" (Suhrke 1977).

Moreover, the Malay language is better and more standardized than it used to be during past decades. These young graduates, using the Arabic texts in their regular teaching, basically explain the Arabic text in standard Malay as it is spoken in Malaysia, occasionally showing some influence of Indonesian accents. This latter happens if the teachers are the graduates of Indonesians universities. Through the effort of the government in upgrading the Thai education in the pondok system of the four southern provinces, the madrasah students gain and master not only the Thai language and Arabic but also Bahasa Malaysia as well. This is due to the fact that the Islamic private schools have been adjusted academically to national and international standards.

Considering the government's policy carefully, therefore one should be delighted with the efforts and the encouragement offered by the government in providing good education to the Malay Muslim children in the South. This is because, with the efforts and the attention being seriously paid to the Muslim education, the students of Islamic private schools now have more options in fields of study at a higher level after graduating from these schools. These schools have discovered how to provide with a challenging

Thai education and an Islamic education to better equip the students for their roles in the governmental and private sectors. On the Islamic side, they have yet to upgrade their standing so that they are at par with the most prestigious academic institutions in Muslim countries, but they have certainly made great strides towards bridging the gap between the aims of the old pondok and the more general ones of Thai education processes.

2. Introducing Thai Education into the Pondok and Creating National Consciousness

It is worthy of observation that the policy of the government in introducing Thai education into the pondok often meets an initial resistance or negative reaction from the religious teachers. For them, Thai education has raised the contentious issue in the fear of the undermining of Muslim faith and this disturbs Muslims generally. With this policy, Islamic education is put under government control. The Muslims think of the policy as a definitive movement towards achieving the goals of Thai nationalism more than anything else. This policy carries certain connotations and has implications beyond what is contained in the words and phrases in which it is written. The real intention of the government lying behind the policy is hard to see. Yet, the educational reform policy for southern Muslims is clearly outlined. What is more, it makes the Muslims of the four southern provinces feel that they have to accomodate themselves to the needs of the situation, if for no other reason than that they have been clearly targeted as a group.

Upgrading the quality of education means more than one can imagine. However, at this stage, the religious teachers feel that they are going to lose their identity in respect to their language, their customs, and their special intellectual system of learning. The government also feels that the difference in language and culture seem to hamper the interaction between the policy of government and the Malay Muslim group, especially in dealing with the matter of compulsory Thai education. Mohammad Abdul Kadir expresses this clearly:

> The existence of this problems is due to the fact that, until very recently, no effective sincere and proper attempt had been made to facilitate communication. Moral instruction, based on Buddhist doctrine, which forms an important part of the curriculum in all categories of academic schools, imposes unacceptable values on people of the Islamic faith.
>
> (Abdul Kadir 1980)

For the reasons mentioned above, many Malay Muslim parents prefer religious schools to Thai academic schools as has been indicated earlier in my discussion. The educational policy of the government, for the country's Malay Muslim parents, seems to carry Thai nationalism beyond what is generally meant by nationalism itself. It is unlikely that the Muslim religious teachers react against the academic training provided by the government, because to obtain knowledge is encouraged by Islam. On principle, they encourage students to obtain more knowledge, so that they can become good citizens of the country. Moreover, learning a language is basically supported by the Prophetic tradition that runs: "Whoever learns the language of a people, he will be saved from their cunning." Hence, the question of the non-participation of the Malay Muslim of the four southern provinces in the educational policy must be reconsidered.

It is not, as has been expressed by some Thai authorities, that the Muslims did not encourage their children to get an education. Should the Thai authorities find it in themselves to understand how strongly the Muslim community adheres to the Islamic faith and how deeply they are committed to Islamic practice and provide a national policy that accords with the Islamic perspective, the educational policies of the government would be well-accepted. In this way, the appropriate response of the government to community sensitivities might create more mutual understanding between the government and the people. Thai government mistreatment of the Muslim in the South can do little more than bring a negative result. That is why parents only send their children to Thai schools in order to finish the compulsory levels of their education. This compulsory education level has recently been extended from four years to six years of schooling.

Furthermore, during the year 1987, a new policy with effect on compulsory education was proposed by the government, thereby extending it from six years to nine years. This proposal is aimed at upgrading the amount of Thai education gained by youth throughout the country. However, it is also aimed directly at getting Malay Muslim children to spend more years in the Thai educational system, with the hope that they will come out with more knowledge and more competence. This policy sounds very attractive on the surface. Nevertheless, it affects the Islamic education received in the Muslim community as a whole. This means that, if the policy is implemented, the children of Muslims have to spend nine years in government compulsory education before transfering to other institutions to study Islam and Arabic offered in more Islamic environments.

It is a fact that the Muslim people in the four southern provinces of Thailand are not satisfied with such a policy. As a result, the religious teachers of the Islamic private schools in the four southern provinces reacted against it. They spoke out, in unity and with clarity that the proposed policy of extending compulsory education from six years to nine years really offends the Muslims of Thailand in the sense that it disturbs the learning of Islam and in the sense there will be no time for Muslim students to study Islam precisely. Besides this, the Islamic education provided in the government schools is not nearly a sufficient substitute. Astri Suhrke describes the schooling situation of the Muslim children in the four southern provinces of Thailand thus:

The Thai government has continuously emphasized that the Muslims must learn the Thai language and receive secular education. Indeed, there is a tendency in Bangkok and among the local government officials to regard education as a panacea for (the) peaceful integration of the Muslims. But the response of the Muslim community to secular education has been mixed. In lower primary school (P.S. 1 - 4, (Thai: Prathom suksa) student enrollment corresponds to the ethnic proportions of the population in the border provinces: Muslims clearly predominate while the Buddhists are a small minority. However, the Muslim student body declines drastically from lower primary to upper primary school (P.S. 5-7) and this trend continues in high school (M.S. 1-3, 4-5, Thai: Mathyom suksa). The overwhelming majority of the student population at these levels is (are) Buddhists, while the Muslims constitute a small minority.

(Suhrke 1977)

This fact is entirely due to the attitudes of the Muslims towards Thai education as previously described. Some Muslim people oppose it because of its contradiction to their traditional values and strongly hold that religious education is more important than Thai education. The fear occurs in the minds of the Muslim people that the Thai government is using secular education to assimilate the Muslims, to make them eventually deny their religion, historical heritage, race and custom (Suhrke 1977). Nantawan Haemindra concurs:

Like other cultural groups, the Muslims are interested in retaining the essence of their traditional culture and fear that the Thai government is trying to assimilate them by changing their local custom, institutions, language and perhaps also religion.

(Haemindra 1977)

They fear this though "it was made clear in the Decree of Religious Toleration, issued by King Chulalongkorn in 1878, that all religions were to be tolerated." (Min. of Nat. Dev. 1965). Fearing that their customs and racial identity, as well as their Malay cultural heritage would be wiped out by the Thai government's policy as it is being introduced through the educational program, the Muslims in the four border provinces now try very hard to preserve that which makes them different form their fellow Thais, both culturally and linguistically. They even think seriously that ... we are ... in a difficult period now because the government is trying to change the Pondok school (Suhrke 1977). Astri Suhrke confirms that:

The pondok has traditionally symbolised the distinct identity of the Malay Muslims as seen by both Muslims and Buddhists. Thai officials have generally considered the pondok as an archaic and reactionary institution that emphasises non-worldly and non-Thai values — an obstacle to development in almost every respect.

(Suhrke 1977)

In addition, the concept of 'Thai' has in practice led Thai officials to define 'Thai-ness' in terms of the language of education (Suhrke 1977). So, if Malay and Arabic are used as the languages of education in the Islamic private schools of Southern Thailand, they will not be considered as Thai. However, considering the advancement of Arabic-religious and Thai programs as well as the reform of educational methods in Islamic private schools of Southern Thailand today, the efforts of the government should be commended, though Astri Suhrke, writing in 1977, considered "that the education policy has failed" (Shurke 1977). Suhrke may well regard the educational policy of the government as a means towards national assimilation. If so, Astri's view than coincides with what Wolf Donner writes in *The Five Faces of Thailand;* he says:

The Thai policy of assimilating minorities has not succeeded with the Muslims, because they have nothing in common: langugage, script, religion, way of living, education and attitudes towards the central government are completely different to those of Thai population.

(Donner 1987)

The education policy of the Thai government makes Malay Muslim feel that their cultural backgrounds are being disturbed. This also makes them suspect the sincerity of the government in the context of educational reform carried out in their community. Thus, the policy has continuously faced negative reaction and resistance from the Muslims, especially at the very first stages of adoption. In fact, as Stephen I. Alpern says,

Any assimilationist policy would focus on educating the Malays in Thai language and culture. But the existing geographical factors, psychological characteristics,... cultural and racial affinities of the Malays are consolidated behind barriers of resistance too strong to overcome in the space of a few generations.

(Alpern 1974)

Some of the attempts made previously by the Thai nation on cultural levels occured after the Thai Revolution of 1932 but, the nationalistic Thai Government tooks its first strong steps toward integration of minority groups in 1939 with the promulgation of the concept of the ... "cultural turtles" (Shrock 1970). A concept embodying their slow but sure incorporation into the nation.

The government, through its educational policy, has tried to regulate the pondok in the four southern provinces and transform them into Islamic private schools. These pondok in previous decades had been more or less ignored by the government. Stepping into the arena of bargaining over policy, the Malay Muslims of the four southern border provinces of Thailand, the religious teachers in particular, have accepted the government policies while maintaining careful eyes in their own concerns. What is done to serve the needs of Muslims in general and without deviating from the fundamentals of Islam, the Muslims will go along with. If any policy appears to lead in the opposite direction, they do their best in order to set the proposed aims on the right course. To this end, they keep on negotiating with the authorities until they can agree on how to handle the issues in a way that will serve the common interests. Their watchful attitude has brought the government to realize that, to make the national policy acceptable, it must cope with the Muslim perspective and that any policy must be acceptable to both sides on its merits; acceptance should not have to be bought by financial inducements. That the government has attempted this, can be seen from the remarks of M. Ladd Thomas when he says:

In the late 1950's the government began to rethink its policy towards these schools, and a decision was eventually reached to encourage them through monetary incentives to first register with the authorities and later convert to private school status.

(Thomas 1969)

In bringing Muslims education into line with the national policy, the government uses every methods they can, including the intervention of local agencies and village leaders to support their plans. The district and provincial officers are important agents in implementing educational programs. The officers involving themselves in Muslim education of southern Thailand believe that they are confronting a non-violent reaction that comes out in the form of adherence to traditional practices. This non-violent reaction expresses more of the Islamic outlook than any consideration of the national needs. The government believes that the Muslim dissatisfaction with the national policy must be solved through various aid programs. On this matter, Stephen I. Alpern writes:

In confronting the educational problem, the Thai government has attempted to persuade Malay religious leaders to align their schools with Thai national educational standards through the use of various forms of inducement, including financial aid, books and other educational materials.

(Alpern 1974)

Solving educational problems through financial aid does not end the complicated demands from the Muslims religious leaders. Such financial aid is not aimed at satisfying the real needs of the people. Rather, the real needs of the Patani Muslims are as fundamentally simple as those found in any Muslim community. That is, education must be carried on in accordance with the needs of the Islamic populace and it must not disrupt the cultural, language and the religious identity of the people. That is why in spite of these attempts to accomodate the needs of Thai Muslims, there remains a strong popular resistance to government education (Alpern 1974).

What is interesting here is that, though the process of changing pondok into Islamic private schools has taken place, indicating the positive response of the Muslims to the education reform policy, many were reluctant to accept either registered or private school status, presumely wishing to teach only non-circular subjects (Thomas 1969).

The Malay Muslims in the region, has looked upon the policy of national education as "the policy of forced cultural assimilation" (Haemindra 1977). Their parents and grandparents had already experienced it in the policy of the late Field-Marshal Phibul Songkram, just prior to and during the Second World War. This was because the "Thai government took its first strong steps towards the cultural integration of minority group in 1939 with the promulgation of the Thai Rathaniyom (Thai Custom Decree)" (Haemindra 1977; Shrock et al. 1970) Uthai Dulyakasem adds that:

... while the 1932 National Education System (of the Thai government) has many important aims, the intention of the government to incorporate politically every religious and ethnic group in the nation apparently was reflected in it.

(Dulyakasem 1981)

Uthai Dulyakasem quotes the National Education system as saying:

1. The State has the right to provide education to the people and the power to supervise education in government schools, local schools and private schools.
2. Compulsory education is the study which the government imposes upon every child without distinction of sex, nationality, and the religion by virtue of the Primary Education Act of 1921.
3. The person who has completed compulsory education is considered to have the knowledge which a Siamese citizen should have, that is to say, he is a citizen who is able to earn his living by having (an) occupation; he knows the rights and duties of the citizen; he will prove himself to be useful for his country by means of his occupation.

(Dulykasem 1981)

Another relevant proclamation is the 1936 National Education Plan. This plan indicates to an even higher degree the national integration policy of the Thai government. The policy says:

The government has the authority to control the institutes, to administer examinations to the teachers and award them diplomas, to administer examinations to students at the completion of Primary General Education, Junior Secondary Education, and Senior Secondary Education.

(Dulykasem 1981)

From the discussion above, it is clear that to have any national policy affecting Thai education implemented effectively, the religion-cultural background and the traditional ways of the people must be carefully respected.

The Emergence of the Madrasah System as a Response to the Challenge

Changing the System to conform to That of the Middle East

The government's introduction of educational reform into the pondok and its efforts to transform the pondok into the Islamic private school gave the idea to the Muslim religious leaders as to how to transform the pondok into the madrasah, a more modern type of Islamic education. With the proper adjustment, they hope that the former (pondok) will remain as it was, while the latter (madrasah) will model and regulate itself in line with the madrasah system of the Muslim countries and those of the Middle East in particular.

It is believed that the religious teachers of Patani who studied the policy of the Thai government have propagated their ideas through new educational institutions known as madrasah, which were modeled after those in Cairo. (Ackerman & Lee 1988).

The particular idea of having the Islamic private school introduced into the pondok as a part of the educational reform proposed by the government touches the essential elements of the traditional education of the pondok. The establishment of the madrasah system in a proper way can not take place immediately nor can its succession be total. The emergence of the madrasah system in the pondok is, actually, an indication of a positive response by the Muslims to the process of change. The procedure of establishing a madrasah system has therefore been carefully prepared and integrated in order to serve the needs of change. Without immediate preparations from the Muslim religious leaders, the pondok system, along its system of Islamic intellectual learning, might disappear from the Muslim community. So, the loosely structured madrasah system of schools has emerged onto the scene as an alert response of the Muslim religious leaders to prepare their schools to comply with the modern trends in education and educational policy, as well as to preserve the tradition of Islamic learning found in the pondok. By doing so, the tok gurus of the pondok in the four southern provinces have adopted the madrasah system of the nearest neighbouring country, Malaysia.

The madrasah system in the pondok during the fifties and the early sixties was very loosely structured and unorganized. The barest educational tools to be found in the pondok were simple blackboards. The students would sit on the floor while attending instruction.

The Muslims in the four southern provinces in their very first modern attempts to get a good education for their children would send them to study at al-Azhar University in Cairo, Egypt. This is due to the fact that al-Azhar University was the first Islamic institution that provided scholarships to

Muslim students from foreign countries, including Thailand. Later on, when opportunities in the Middle East opened up further, increasing the chances of getting a scholarship, they would send their children to study in other Middle Eastern countries, such as the Kingdom of Saudi Arabia, Iraq, Kuwait, Sudan, Libya, Tunisia, Morocco and Algeria. This educational trend has occured among the young Muslims of Thailand in general and those of Patani in particular. They have gravitated towards those countries specifically because the Muslim parents wanted their children to learn proper Islamic theology and Arabic language. By sending their students to study in these countries, it is hoped that the young Muslims will also bring back up-to-date methods of teaching to the transformed madrasah of Patani. Hence, sending some of the most promising students to acquire a proper knowledge of Islam and Arabic from these Middle Eastern countries becomes an important thing. The Muslim parents hope that the madrasah systems of Patani will be taught along the same lines of those of the Middle Eastern countries.

During the period of preparation for the change, due to the lack of qualified personnel in the field, Muslim religious teachers are aware of the need to carefully adjust from the old system (pondok) into the modern system (madrasah). That is to say, they require that the madrasah system be introduced into the pondok in order to serve the needs of the modern times. At the same time, they demand that the old system of traditional Islamic heritage be retained and taught in the pondok as it has been for decades gone by.

The students who are sent to study in the Muslim countries and especially those in the Middle Eastern universities, either from the pondok system or from the loosely transformed madrasah, also need to catch up academically in the subjects taught in the madrasah system. In doing so, these students have to spend several years in the madrasah system in an Arab country learning those neglected subjects. These subjects provide them with the sort of well-rounded view of academic learning that will lead them to continue their studies at the university level in their field of interest. As a result, they can enter study at the university level after obtaining high school certificate in those countries. The students who are capable of studying sciences (*qism al-'ulûm*) and show competency are allowed to follow two lines of study, such as those that are offered by Ma'had al-Qâhirah, al-Azhar University, Cairo, Egypt. They can then continue their education, not only in the Faculty of Shariah and Law, the Faculty of Usul al-Din, the Faculty of Islamic Studies or the Faculty of Arabic, but also can proceed in other faculties which are related to the science stream. This new phenomenon, in fact, began mainly in the late fifties and sixties.

However from the seventies to the present time the situation has changed. The fact is that the religious teachers of Patani have carefully adopted the policy of the government and included Thai education, including educational in general subjects, in the madrasah (formerly pondok), whose name has latterly changed to the Islamic private school. As a result of this adoption, the students at the Islamic private school have received two types of education, i.e., the Arabic-religious and Thai educations. The Thai education includes, generally, two lines of study: sciences and arts, along with vocational themes. The students who study in the sciences can therefore easily further their study in faculties dealing with the sciences if they are sent to study in the Middle Eastern countries.

Within the national system of higher education, the students of the Islamic private school are unrestricted in choosing their fields of study, provided they pass the University Entrance Exam. This allows the students of the Islamic private school of today to have more opportunities than their contemporaries of the late fifties and sixties in university enrolment, either in Thailand or in the Muslim countries. The universities in the Muslim countries recommend that, to study at the university level, students obtain both Arabic-religious and Thai general certificate. This opens to them a greater variety of university programs of study instead of their conditional enrollment in only the Arabic-religious programs. The students can also follow different fields of study in other faculties like Science, Commerce, Education, Languages and Medicine.

Although the process of change has taken place in the pondok, the traditional learning in the pondok does not decrease its major role in providing Islamic education to the students and to the community at large. Rather, the pondok, in its role as an Islamic learning center, plays two significant parts: the traditional learning part and the modern system that complies exactly with the changing process. In other words, the new method of learning has been included while the traditional education has been kept alive. This is partly because the education provided in the pondok is the type of informal education by which one can acquire Islamic knowledge throughout one's lifetime. It is worth mentioning here that the responses of the Muslims toward the process of change seem unique. This uniqueness appears in the form of the "Persatuan Sekolah Agama Rakyat" in Malay, which they called in Arabic "Ittihâd al-Madâris al-Islâmîyah al-Ahlîyah" (The Association of Islamic Private Schools). This Persatuan Sekolah Agama Rakyat involves itself only in matters concerning Arabic-religious curriculum and directly serves the madrasah system. Under the Persatuan Sekolah Agama Rakyat, the madrasah lay out their Arabic-religious curriculum and syllabus of teaching. In order to conform with the *madrasah* of other Muslim countries, the madrasah of Patani are systematically divided into three levels; al-marhalah *al-ibtidâ'îyah* (the six-year elementary level), al-marhalah *al-mutawassitah* (the three-year middle level), and al-marhalah al-*thânawîyah* (the three-year secondary level). The six-year elementary level is usually reduced in Thailand to four years. The reasoning behind this is that most of the Muslim children have already studied how to read the Quran and also familiarized themselves with Arabic and Jawi writing while they have been attending the *tadika* school. This *tadika* education can replace the first two years of elementary level provided in the madrasah, in which case the children usually enter the madrasah at the third year of *al-ibtidâ'îyah* level without any difficulty. The curriculum established by the Persatuan Sekolah Agama Rakyat (The Association of Islamic Private Schools) has already been recognized by Muslim institutions abroad.

The Curriculum

The following are the levels of study and the subjects taught in the madrasah in the four southern provinces. This plan of study is that prescribed by The Association of Islamic Private Schools (Tables 5.2, 5.3 and 5.4).

Examining the subjects provided in the madrasah of Patani, it is clear that its curriculum is designed to be acceptable to and accredited by similar academic institutions and educational authorities in Middle Eastern countries. Thus, any madrasah of the same quality and character and providing the same levels of study will be recognized by those universities and authorities. This means that a student with a secondary certificate (*Shahâdat al-thânawîyah*) is actually qualified to enter the first year of university level in any of these countries. In fact, many Arabic schools of the modern madrasah system in the four southern provinces are accredited by the Ministry of Education of the Kingdom of Saudi Arabia (Fig 5.1).

The madrasah in the four southern provinces whose level of teaching has reached the level of that provided in the Islamic University of Medina, Saudi Arabia, or other representative institutions in Middle Eastern countries, might likely be recognized by either the Ministry of Education of that country or by the Academy Department, Ministry of Awqâf.

It should be noted here that such recognition where granted, has been achieved through the Arabic-religious curriculum and within the madrasah institution. Other examples of accredited schools would be Ma'had al 'Ulûm for Pondok Jerang Batu, Patani, Ma'had al-Tarbîyah for Pondok Bana, Patani, Madrasah Azizstan for Pondok Naprado, Patani, and Markaz al-Dirâsât al-Islâmîyah al-Âliyah, for Pondok Chumae, Saiburi, Patani. The names of pondok and those of the "Islamic private school," which are officially given in Thai, might not be formally used when making contact with the Middle Eastern institutions. In other words, the Arabic name which is given to the pondok or the Islamic private school is the only expression that carries its Islamic and cultural message to the Muslim word. It is no fable that most of the Islamic private schools in the four southern provinces bear three different names. The first and the most well-known name is that of the pondok, which might designated either by the name of its founder or its location. The second one is the madrasah or similar institutional tittle. In this

Subjek: Statement of Equivalence of Ma'had a;-Ulûm
1/4 Tambun Rusembilan Patani, Thailand

The Kingdom of Saudi Arabia,
Ministry of Education

Curriculum:

al-Tafsîr (Interpretation of Quran)
*al-Taw*h*îd* (Islamic Theology)
al-Fiqh (Islamic Jurisprudence)

1. Elementary level 6 years
2. Middle level 3 years
3. Secondary level 3 years

The resolution no 54/401 dated on 11/11/1401 A.H. (1981 A.D.) was as follows:

1. The Middle Certificate qualifies the student to enter the first year of the secondary school of the Islamic University.

2. The Secondary Certificate qualifies the student to enter the first year in one of the colleges of the Islamic University, with the exception of the College of the Holy Quran.

The Islamic University, Medina
The Kingdom of Saudi Arabia

Figure 5.1 Recognition Certificate issued by the Ministry of Education,
the Kingdom of Saudi Arabia at the Islamic University in Medina
(translated by the author)

case, it is very common for the people to use a Malay word 'sekolah' (school) to refer to the madrasah itself. Again, when the word 'sekolah', is used, the name of its location is mentioned in vernacular dialect. That is to say, the Ma'had al-Tarbîyah al-Dînîyah, Bana, Patani, is refered to as Sekolah Bana or Sekolah Haji Yusoh (Yusof), and Ma'had al-Ulum is called Sekolah Baba Teh (Abd al-Latif) or Sekolah Jerang Batu. The third name, which is officially given to each registered pondok, is rarely mentioned by the students, let alone the common people. It is the name which officially designates the institution as an Islamic private school. This official name, some sort of a mixture of Thai and corrupt Arabic, seems to be used only when it is necessary for an official mention.

The middle Eastern countries identify the Islamic private schools of Patani through their Arabic names. The term chosen might be *ma'had* (institute), madrasah (school), *mu'assasah* (institute, foundation) or *markaz* (center).

TABLE 5.2 The Plan of Study for al-Marḥalah al-ibtidâ'îyah (Elementary Level)

Subjects/Levels	Total of Study Periods per Week *Majmû' al-Ḥiṣaṣ fi-al-Usbu'*					
	1	2	3	4	5	6
al-Ulûm al-Dînîyah (Religious subjects)						
1. *al-Qur'ân al-Karîm*	6	6	5	2	2	2
2. *al-Tajwîd* (Quranic Chanting)	-	-	1	1	1	1
3. *al-Tafsîr* (Quran Commentary)	-	-	-	2	2	2
4. *al-Hadîth* (Prophetic Tradition)	-	-	-	2	2	2
5. *al-Tawḥid* (Islamic Theology)	3	3	2	2	2	2
6. *al-Fiqh* (Islamic Jurisprudence)	3	3	2	2	2	2
al-Ulûm al-Lughawîyah (Linguistics)						
a. *al-'Arabîyah* (Arabic)						
7. *al-Naḥw* (Grammar	-	-	1	1	2	2
8. *al-Ṣarf* (Morphology)	-	-	1	1	1	1
9. *al-Muṭâla'ah* (Comprehension)	3	3	2	2	2	2
10. *al-Ta'bîr* (Expression)	-	-	1	1	1	1
11. *al Imlâ'* (Dictation)	3	3	2	2	2	2
12. *al-Khaṭṭ* (Handwriting)	2	2	1	1	1	1
13. *al-Muḥâdathah* (Conversation)	-	-	1	1	1	1
14. *al-Maḥfûẓât* (Memorization)	-	-	1	1	1	1
b. *al-Malâyûwîyah* (Malay)						
15. *al-Qirâ'ah* (Reading)	2	2	2	1	1	1
16. *al-Imlâ* (Dictation)	2	2	2	2	1	1
17. *al-Inshâ'* (Composition)	2	2	2	2	2	2
al-'Ulûm al-Ijtimâ'îyah (Social Sciences)						
18. *al-Sîrah al-Nabawîyah*						
(Life of Muhammad)	2	2	2	2	2	2
19. *al-Akhlâq* (Ethics)	2	2	2	2	2	2
Total	30	30	30	30	30	30

Textbooks and the Language of Teaching

The books used in the madrasah as texts are imported mostly from the Muslim countries, Middle Eastern countries in particular. Some are produced by the ulama of Patani and others have been written by the Malaysian ustaz (teachers). The Local Arabic textbooks which are taught in the madrasah system have been written primarily by a number Patani modernist ustaz, such as Ustaz Haji Abd al-Latif bin Haji Wan Muhammad Nur, Tok Guru

TABLE 5.3 The Plan of Study for *al-Marḥalah al-Mutawassiṭah* (Middle Level)

Total of Study Periods per Week *Majmû' al-Ḥiṣaṣ fi-al-Usbu'*			
Subjects/Level	1	2	3
al-'Ulûm al-Dînîyah			
1. *al-Qur'ân al-Karim*	2	2	2
2. *al-Tafsîr*	2	2	2
3. *al-Ḥadîth*	2	2	2
4. *al-Tawḥîd*	2	2	2
5. *al-Fiqh*	2	2	2
6. *al-Farâ'iḍ* (Inheritance)	1	1	1
al-'Ulûm al-Lughawîyah			
a. *al-'Arabîyah*			
7. *Qawâ'id al-Lughah al-'Arabîyah*	4	4	4
(Rules of Arabic Grammar)			
8. *al-Muṭâla'ah*	2	2	2
9. *al-Inshâ'*	2	2	2
10. *al-Adab al-'Arabî* (Literature)	1	1	1
11. *al-Balâghah* (Rhetoric)	-	1	1
12. *al-Khaṭṭ*	1	-	-
13. *al-Imlâ'*	1	1	1
14. *al-Muḥâdathah*	2	2	2
b. *al-Malâyûwîyah*			
15. *al-Qirâ'ah*	1	1	1
16. *al-Imlâ'*	1	1	1
17. *al-Insha'*	1	1	1
al-'Ulûm al-Ijtimâ'îyah			
18. *al-Ta'rîkh al-Islâmî* (Islamic History)	2	2	2
19. *al-Akhlâq*	1	1	1
Total	30	30	30

of Madrasah Ma'had al-Ulum, Jerang Batu, Patani, Ustadh Haji Wan Yusuf Musa al-Bandari, Tok Guru of Ma'had al-Tarbîyah al-Dînîyah, Bana, Patani, Haji Abd al-Rahman Ahmad, Tok Guru of Mu'assasah al-Thaqâfah al-Islâmîyah, Pombing, Patani and Dr. Haji Ismail Lutfi, the Ustaz of Madrasah al-Rahmânîyah, Pujud, Patani. These modernists, among others, have written Arabic textbooks in order to serve the needs of the students in the madrasah system. During recent years, imported textbooks, which are being used in the typical madrasah of Patani, are produced either by the

TABLE 5.4. The Plan of Study for *al-Marḥalah al-Thânawîyah* (Secondary Level)

Total of Study Periods per Week *Majmû' al-Ḥiṣaṣ fi-al-Usbu'*

Subjects/Levels	1	2	3
al-'Ulûm al-Dînîyah			
1. *al-Qur'ân al-Karîm*	1	1	1
2. *al-Tafsîr*	2	2	2
3. *Uṣûl al-Tafsîr* (Principles of Qur'ânic Commentary)	1	1	1
4. *al-Ḥadîth*	3	3	3
5. *Muṣṭalah al-Ḥadîth* (Hadîth Criticism)	1	1	-
6. *al-Fiqh*	2	2	2
7. *Uṣûl al-Fiqh*	2	2	2
8. *al-Qawâ'id al-Fiqhîyah* (Principles of Fiqh)	-	1	2
9. *al-Falsafah al-Islâmîyah* (Islamic Philosophy)	-	1	1
10. *Ta'rîkh al-Tashrî'*	2	2	2
11. *Ḥikmat al-Tashrî'* (Wisdom of Islamic Law)	1	1	-
12. *Mabâdi' fi al-Fiqh al-Muqâran* (Introduction to Comparative Islamic Jurisprudence)	-	1	2
13. *al-Tawḥîd*	2	2	2
al-'Ulûm al-Lughawiyah			
14. *Qawâ'id al-Lughah al-'Arabîyah*	2	2	2
15. *al-Inshâ'*	2	1	1
16. *al-Nuṣûṣ al-'Adabîyah* (Arabic Literature)	1	1	1
17. al-Balâghah	1	1	1
18. *al-Lughah al-Malâyûwîyah*	2	1	1
19. *al-Lughah al-Injilîzîyah* (English)	1	1	1
al-'Ulûm al-Ijtimâ'îyah			
20. *al-Ta'rîkh al-Islâmîyah* (Islamic History)	2	1	1
21. *al-Thaqâfah al-Islâmîyah* (Islamic Culture)	2	2	2
Total	30	30	30

Sources: Curricula of Sasnupatam School-Bana, Patani, South Thailand

Ministry of Education, the Kingdom of Saudi Arabia or King Sa'ud University, Riyadh. These textbooks are supplied to some madrasah of Patani as educational donations, to be used there after in the madrasah of Patani and in Thailand as a whole.

Considering the textbooks used in the madrasah throughout the four southern provinces, it is clear that the language of teaching in the madrasah is primarily Arabic, while Malay operates as a linguistic counterpart. This is because the textbooks are in Arabic and Malay is used as the means to understand the Arabic texts. The Malay language is the daily language of the people of these areas. Therefore, it is apparent that the Malay language is important in functioning as the language of interpretation to all students to access and understand the texts. In this case, the Malay language plays a significant role, side-by-side with the Arabic, especially at the elementary level. The higher the level of the students then the lesser the Malay language functions. This means that when the students attain the secondary level (*al-Marhalah al-Thânawîyah*), Arabic becomes the medium of instruction. To understand the Arabic texts, the teachers (ustaz) have to use standard Arabic and find the simplest way to interpret the Arabic texts using the original language. So, the students automatically learn standard forms of Arabic. In the case of colloquial Arabic, the students learn only a very few such expression from their teachers. Such colloquial Arabic expressions vary in dialect and may also be restricted in accent contexts as well, depending on the educational background of the modernists (ustaz) themselves. If they are graduates of the Egyptian universities, then their expressions tend to be in an Egyptian dialect and if they are the graduates of Saudi Arabian universities then their expressions are delivered in a Saudi dialect and so on. It is interesting to note at this point that neither Thai expression nor Thai translation are involved in the Arabic-religious teaching found in Islamic private schools. The Thai language will never supercede the Malay language. Through this system, students whose mother tongue is not Malay may also have the chance to learn the Malay language from the juniors and seniors as well as from their teachers. These are the features of the Islamic private schools in the four southern provinces.

The Islamic private schools in Region Two are numerous, not to mention those that are established in Regions Three and Four. They are found scattered in Patani, Yala, Narathiwat and Satun. There are many Islamic private schools scattered over the four southern border provinces, Educational Region Two. These schools represent, directly or indirectly, those of Regions Three and Four. What should be borne in mind is that the Arabic names given to these schools are mixed with the Thai language in a corrupt or distorted form. Some names are also combined with place names and Malay dialect words referring to those areas, while yet others are written purely in the Thai language. Whatever official names have been given to these madrasahs or Islamic private schools, their common names in Arabic will not be distorted, for the religious teachers know how to name their madrasahs in the correct way, according to relevant Islamic and Arabic terms. The distortion of these names mentioned earlier occurred when the government started to try and improve the status of pondok and to have them registered under stricter and more formalised government control. This was the beginning of the matter. The names of those madrasahs (i.e., the Arabic names written in Arabic language) were then totally altered when the pondok were transformed into the Islamic private schools, accepting Thai education as a step to help the pondok survive. At the office of registration, the Arabic names were corrupted and these corrupt Arabic names became the official names referring to the Arabic schools of these regions. No one knows whether the names were intentionally corrupted during the registration process or whether it was done without any awareness by those authorities and individuals who took responsibility for naming the madrasahs. Nevertheless, the feeling of attempted prescriptive assimilation and integration is further culturally and linguistically etched in the minds of the Muslim people of Patani. As a matter of fact, it is not so difficult to transcribe Arabic names in Thai and still retain the correct forms so that the sound word or name almost exactly follows the original.

Looking through the educational levels provided in the Islamic private schools, we notice that there are more elementary (Ibtidâ'îyah) and middle (Mutawassiṭah) level schools than secondary (Thânawîyah) schools. However, with time, the lower levels may be changed and upgraded into higher levels.

Another important fact that should be brought out here is that the Islamic private school that does not include Thai education in its program cannot get subsidies or support from the government. So, the owner of such a school may have to expend much more effort in order to keep the school on a sound financial footing. In these circumstances, several of the Islamic private schools, so unsubsidised have already closed.

An explanation of Thai terminology for educational levels would be in order here. That is to say, the Thai education provided by the Islamic private schools encompasses several levels of teaching. Each level carries certain abbreviations. For example: the "k. 3-4" level (Thai: Karnsuksa pujai, adult education), indicate a non-formal educations program. The "k.3" level indicates the levels of compulsory education from which a student earns the certificate of elementary education as soon as he passes the final examination, while the "k. 4" level shows the levels of education after which a student obtains the certificate of lower education at his final examination.

Similar to the above categories, the level "r. 3-4" (Thai: Radap karnsuksa, another type of adult education), is also offered. The "M. 1-3" level (Thai: Mathyomton, lower secondary level) indicates a formal educational program, at the conclusion of which the student receives his lower secondary certificate of education. The higher secondary certificate starts from the "M. 4-6" level (Thai: Mathyomprai, higher secondary level) during which the student spends three years finishing his studies. We find that a few Islamic private schools offer Thai education from "M. 1-6" level. However, there are twelve schools providing a complete program in Thai education, as well as the Arabic-religious program:

1. Attarqiyah Islamiyyah, Narathiwat Province.
2. Darunsat Vitya, Saiburi District, Patani Province.
3. Saiburi Islam Vitya, Saiburi District, Patani Province.
4. Sansnupatham, Muang District, Patani Province.
5. Azizstan, Kokpo District, Patani Province.
6. Satri Patnasuksa, Muang District, Patani Province.
7. Phattana Vitya, Muang District, Yala Province.
8. Thamvitya, Amphao Muang, Yala Province.
9. Phattanakarnsuksa, Muang District, Satun Province.
10. Dârul Ma'ârif, Kuandon District, Satun Province.
11. Saengprathip, Muang District, Satun Province.
12. Mamba'ul 'Ulûm, Muang District, Satun Province.

The fact is that these schools have taken strong steps towards aligning their systems with both the educational policy of the government and those of the Muslim countries. They stand firmly as a pattern for other Islamic private schools in the region, producing qualified students who are able to continue their education with the higher academic learning that the nation needs.

CHAPTER 6

Central Government Efforts

Establishing Educational Region Two in Yala and Direct Contact with the Pondok Founders

In order to make national policy more effective, in the early 1950's the government established a General Education Development Center in Yala (Alpern 1974) known as Educational Region Two. The main objective of establishing the Center was 'the need for good (Thai) language instruction programs' and to create a cooperative agency that would function to link the government and the Muslim institutions of the southern provinces of Thailand. Educational Region Two was destined to take serious responsibility to help improve the Islamic private schools in the four border provinces.

In fact, the efforts of the center have met a largely positive but cautious reaction from the Muslim communities in those areas. This is because the coordinators and the personnel working in the center are mostly Muslims, and they deal directly with the local Muslim leaders and make them their consultants in implementing proposed projects. The coordinator, in their turn, also listen to the suggestions made by the local Muslim leaders.

The General Education Center located in the town of Yala began to pay special attention to the Thai-Islam (sic) by the end of that decade and by the mid-1960's was heavy preoccupied with devising means for getting more of them into primary school (Thomas 1969). The aim of this Center, using several devices, is to bring Malay Muslim children into Thai education and, in the first stage of its work, it hoped to turn one of the Islamic religious schools (now a private school) into a model for others by improving Thai language and other secular instruction (Thomas 1969).

Educational Region Two also uses new methods of teaching Thai language to the Malay children in their earliest years in the public school. This involves designing special teaching techniques and textbook materials, holding in-service training courses to acquaint teachers with these and operating several demonstration classes at the first grade level (Thomas 1969).

Another activity provided by the Center is holding numerous seminars for education officials, teacher and tok gurus (religious teachers) in the Islamic schools) on ways of resolving difficulties attending upon the teaching of Thai-Islam (sic) students in public and private schools (Thomas 1969).

Upgrading Pondok Status and Introducing Islamic Studies Program into the Curriculum of the Public Elementary School

Community reaction has not been positive everywhere however. Rung Kaewdaeng, in his 1968 study on "The Attitude of Religious Teachers towards the Reformation of the Pondok into the Islamic private School" in Educational Region Two, concluded that a majority of tok gurus thought that the pondok system should not be reformed. One reason was that they did not understand the 1954/2497 B.E (Kaewdaeng 1968) Regulation of the Private School. Another reason is that the tok gurus did not realize certain, specific privileges of the Islamic private schools which were (and are) different from those of the private school in general. In fact the Islamic private schools receive both academic and monetary support from the government. In these circumstances, Kaewdaeng reports, the tok gurus felt that the 1961 reform process directed at the pondok might decrease the rights they were used to enjoying, (Kaewdaeng 1968) such as their position as principal of the pondok and as its owner. They feared losing their positions because the 1954 Regulation of the Private School required that the principal of the pondok must obtain at least the lower certificate of education in Thai. Most of them had no such qualification and would experience enormous difficulties in obtaining one.

Acharn Manich Charong, a high-ranking Muslim of the Educational Region Two, is working hard to implement the policy of the Center. He faces a number of problems in initial attempts to introduce Thai education into the pondok. During the first step of the process, he has personally realized how thick the wall of defenses built out of Muslim tradition is. He has worked hard to make them understand the real purpose of the project. He has received strong resistance and negative reactions from some tok gurus during the first attempts. Mr. Charong continuously visits tok gurus and explains to them the advantages of the new policy. At last, the policies are being accepted and the Thai education program in the pondok is in progress. As a Muslim, born a Thai in the Malay Muslim community, Charong hopes to see the academic programs of the pondok align with the rest of the Thai education system, without detracting from its roots and systems of Arabic-religious education.

The first task of this Center, one that also affects madrasah systems, is to introduce Thai education into the traditional institutions. As a result, the title of pondok has been officially changed into that of the "Islamic private school", as it is today. The acceptance of educational reform policy by the tok gurus brings good will from the government and also from the executive personnel of Educational Region Two. At the same time, the tok gurus learn how to adjust their institution to conform with the new policy.

The second task of the Center, specified in those early days, was to bring Islamic teaching to the public schools. Acharn Manich Charong is also now head of the Islamic studies project at the elementary school level. He is responsible for providing Islamic studies in the public schools of the five southern provinces.

It is understandable that the Muslims, as a whole, like to send their children to receive a religious education in the pondok. Unless Islamic education is included in public schools, the tendency to send Muslim children towards more religiously-oriented institutions will continue.

Due in the main to his long experience, Mr. Charong has been appointed to run the program. He labors very hard in order to make the program run smoothly and to have it effectively implemented in public schools. The first phase of the project is to offer Islamic program at the elementary level. If the project is adequate and impressive, then the program will be introduced at the secondary level. It is expected through this effort that the students will receive the opportunity to learn more about Islam and its daily practices, as well as to know what is right and what is wrong according to Islamic principles.

When tracing the history of the Islamic studies program offered in the public schools of the five southern border provinces, it should be noted that in 1975 the Ministry of Education received a mandate to teach *Islamic studies* in public elementary schools in the five southern provinces. Considering the importance of religious studies, *the office of the Educational Inspector*, Region Two, drafted a curriculum for Islamic studies at the elementary level and submitted it to the Ministry of Education in 1976. Consequently, on June 7, 1976, the Ministry of Education approved the curriculum that includes the following subjects:

1. The foundation of faith (*tawhîd*)
2. Islamic precepts (*fiqh*)
3. Religious history (*târîkh*)
4. al-Quran
5. The art of Quranic chanting (*tajwîd*)
6. Arabic
7. Ethics (*akhlâq*)

The teaching in the very first phase of the project was intended to be conducted by Muslim teachers in extracurricular hours outside of the regular school periods.

Initially, the effort did not win the full support of the administrators of schools, districts and provinces. So the Islamic teaching program almost failed before it had had a chance to function properly.

In the year 1978, the National Security Council urged that the security of the southern border provinces in every aspect be supported appropriately. With a view to the socio-psychological aspects of public education, the National Security Council suggested that Islam be taught to Muslim children at elementary, middle, secondary, vocational, teachers' college, and university levels. The cabinet approved the suggestion and the National Security Council launched the operation. As a result, The Office of Educational Inspector, Region Two, was given the responsibility of acquiring the requisite number of teachers and training them to the level at which they could teach Islam in accordance with the Islamic curriculum prescribed in 1976.

Due to the changing of the elementary public school year enrollment system from seven grades to six grades, the revised curriculum of Islamic studies in the elementary level was also changed. The subjects covered in Islamic studies were there after reduced from seven to five. The subjects retained were *tawhîd*, *fiqh*, *târîkh*, *akhlâq*, and al-Quran. This was done in order to make the subjects more appropriate to the ages and the levels of the pupils. Accordingly, on 13 November 1981, the Ministry of Education approved the revised curriculum of Islamic studies.

It is worth mentioning here that the teaching of Islam in the elementary schools is done under the supervision of three governmental organizations: (1) The Office of the National Elementary Education Committee, (2) The Office of the Regional Inspector, Educational Region Two, and (3) The Office of Provincial Elementary Educational for five southern provinces (Matyusof 1985).

The objectives of the Islamic teaching project in the elementary schools of the five southern border provinces can now be outlined as follows:

1. To effectively encourage the teaching of Islam in the elementary schools of the southern border provinces in accordance with the policy of the government.
2. To encourage the people of the southern border provinces to pay more attention to education, and to appreciate the educational institution that might incite them to send more of their children to the public schools and to higher education.
3. To inspire students to learn both Islamic subjects and Thai or vocational studies, so that they may acquire sufficient knowledge and become capable of using the Thai language (Matyusof 1985).

The response of the government, in fact, satisfied Muslim parents, with the reciprocal effect that the Islamic studies subjects be introduced into the higher levels of the government schools, so that Muslim children could go on to learn more about Islam and Islamic ethics. This further encouraged parents who were pleased with the actions taken by the authorities, as well as the school administrators. This was because the students could learn Islam and perform their daily prayers at school without having any difficulty. The parents also appreciated the fact that a prayer place (Arabic: *muṣallâ*, Malay: tempat sembahyang) was added to school buildings as a special provision.

The Muslim parents then suggested that the teachers responsible for teaching Islam must be of good character and must be qualified in the field in which they are teaching. They should be examples, not only for the students but also for the community at large.

According to Mr. Charong, the head of the Islamic studies project in the elementary schools for the five southern border provinces, the process of having Islamic studies subjects introduced into the public schools has achieved a great success. Mr. Charong hopes to see the project continue to serve the Muslim children up to the higher level. Mr. Charong also expects to receive appreciation and understanding from his community and would appreciate feedback and constructive criticism, so that the aims of providing Islamic education in the public schools will be effectively fulfilled. According to the research conducted by the division of the "Teaching Islam in Elementary School Project", it is clear that the Muslim parents in the five southern border provinces are satisfied with the project as it has been supported by the government. They find themselves aligned with the government because of this positive responses and furthermore they find the Islamic studies subjects beneficial in providing moral education for their children.

Producing Syllabus, Curriculum and Textbooks for the Islamic Private School

In the Office of Educational Region Two there is another division whose function: to take responsibility for the Islamic private schools; beginning with the curriculum, syllabus and plan of study and ending with the production of Arabic textbooks for the students. This division is under the direction of Acharn Arom Mamah and his staff. This group is working towards gearing the Islamic private school up to the standard of learning and teaching proposed by the government. Because of the Thai education introduced into the Islamic private school, the period of teaching and the curriculum of both Arabic-religious and Thai education have to be adjusted to fit the capabilities of the students. The two types of education are not offered at the same time during a school day, rather, religious education takes place in the morning while the Thai education usually starts at one o'clock in the afternoon.

According to the concept of the Thai authorities as it maybe reviewed through Thai documents, the textbooks used in the Islamic private schools of the four southern provinces are also the sources of problems. The reason is that imported textbooks written by foreigners may not fully serve the needs of the students and are also viewed as having the potential to attract the Muslim students to those countries. Another reason is that imported texts are expensive and it would be better to have the textbooks produced by qualified educated Muslims native to the country and published in the country.

To help solve the problem of the textbooks effectively, the Ministry of Education of Thailand has a mandate to publish curriculum texts of the four-year elementary level (al-Marhalah al-Ibtidâ'îyah), curriculum texts of the three-year middle level (al-Marhalah al-Mutawassitah) and curriculum texts of the three-year secondary level (al-Marhalah al-Thânawîyah). These documents were to be introduced by the executive personnel of Educational Region Two. To have the curricula and related text introduced effectively, the executive personnel of the Office of Educational Region Two recommended that the textbooks be produced in a form relating to the local situation to properly serve the levels of learning in an Islamic private school. The concrete ideas proposed by the executive personnel, resulting from several meetings and seminars held for that purpose, were accepted and the executive committee of the Office of Educational Region Two appointed fifty qualified educational personnel, headed by Dr. Chaeng Sukhkua, the then inspector of Educational Region Two as members of the groups drafting the curriculum and related materials.

The personnel who were then responsible for the Arabic-religious curricula in the Islamic private school were the religious teachers from the leading Islamic private schools in Regions Two, Three, and Four. Four Muslim judges, *tok qadi* (Malay-Thai: *datok yuttitham*) from Patani, Yala, Narathiwat and Satun provinces were also included. These members of the drafting committee were mostly graduated of Middle Eastern universities.

In a sense, they are the modernists, the well-versed teachers in Arabic, known in the Muslim community as ustaz. Most of them are the Arabic religious teachers for those schools. With their efforts and their energy and under the guidance of the office of Educational Region Two, the Arabic religious textbooks are now written and produced. The textbooks for all such subjects are written in Arabic, but some explanations are to be found in Malay. The Ministry of Education allocated a special budget to cover the huge expenses of having these texts produced in forms suited to standards approved by the government and finally, the completed curricula and materials of the Islamic private school were published and introduced.

The following tables present the Arabic-religious curricula and the subjects assigned by the Office of Educational Region Two, Ministry of Education. These curricula are being used in the Islamic private schools in the four southern provinces. The curricula are divided into three groups as shown in Tables 6.1, 6.2 and 6.3.

These tables indicate the subjects and periods of teaching as well as the curricula provided by the Islamic private schools in the four southern border

TABLE 6.1 The Arabic-Religious Curriculum at the Elementary
Level (Ibtidâ'îyah) in the Year 1980/2523 B.E.

Subjects	Total Periods per Week			
	Level 1	Level 2	Level 3	Level 4
Religion				
1. Quran	5/8	5/8	4/7	4/7
2. Religious activities	4	4	4	4
3. *Tawhîd*	3	2	2	2
4. *Fiqh*	3	2	2	2
5. *Tajwîd*	-	-	1	1
Languages				
a. Arabic				
6. *Nahw*	-	1	2	2
7. *Sarf*	-	1	1	1
8. *Mutâla'ah*	2	2	2	2
9. *Imlâ'*	2	2	1	1
10. *Inshâ'*	-	1	1	1
11. *Muhâdathah*	3	2	2	2
12. *Khatt*	1	1	1	1
13. *Adab/Nusûs*	-	-	1	1
b. Malay/or Quran	3/0	3/0	3/0	3/0
Social Studies				
14. *Ta'rîkh al-Islâm*	2	2	2	2
15. *Akhlâq*	2	2	1	1
Total	30	30	30	30

provinces. They are officially approved by the Ministry of Education. All of the Islamic private schools in the four southern provinces today use these curricula, as well as the books that are produced by the Office of Educational Region Two and published by the Ministry of Education. However, some additional textbooks are utilized to supplement the approved curricula. These additional texts are chosen for the students of middle and secondary levels. These texts are generally selected from the lists of publishers in the Middle Eastern countries. These texts are chosen by the teachers who want to train their students to be familiar with the styles and contexts of the original Arabic texts, written by mother tongue speakers of the Arabic language. Without giving the students special training in standard Arabic textbooks or making them familiar with the styles and systems of learning in those countries, the

TABLE 6.2 The Arabic Religious Curriculum at the Middle
Level (Mutawassiṭah) in the Year 1980/2523 B.E.

Subject	Total Periods per Week		
	Level 1	Level 2	Level 3
Religion			
1. Quran	2/5	2/5	2/5
2. *Tafsîr*			
3. *Ḥadîth*	2	2	2
4. *Tawḥîd*	2	2	2
5. *Fiqh*	2	2	2
6. *Fara'iḍ*	1	1	1
Languages			
a. Arabic			
7. *Quwâ'id al-'Arabîyah*	4	4	4
8. *Muṭâla'ah*	2	2	2
9. *Inshâ'*	2	2	2
10. *Adab/Nuṣûṣ*	1	1	1
11. *Balâghah*	-	1	1
12. *Khaṭṭ*	1	1	1
13. *Imlâ'*	1	1	1
14. *Muḥâdathah*	2	2	2
b. Malay/or Quran	3/0	3/0	3/0
Social Studies			
15. *Ta'rîkh al-Islâm*	2	2	2
16. *Akhlâq*	1	1	1
Total	30	30	30

students from the Islamic private schools may face problems with those
systems if they are ever fortunate enough to be sent to study in those
countries.

Another reason is that if the students fail to be competitive in the Middle
Eastern universities when they eventually study in them, the Islamic private
schools (actually the madrasah system) where they obtained their secondary
certificate will automatically lose their accreditation by official agencies in
the Arab World. Consequently, their schools may not receive any scholarships
from Middle Eastern universities or their financial and from those sources
may be terminated. These are further justification as to why the Arabic-

TABLE 6.3 The Arabic-Religious Curriculum at the Secondary
Level (Thânawîyah) in the Year 1980/2523 B.E.

Subjects	The Periods per Week					
	Level 1		Level 2		Level 3	
	C.	E.	C.	E.	C.	E.
Religion						
1. Quran	4/2	-	4/2	-	3/2	-
2. *Hadîth*	2	2	2	2	2	-
3. *Fiqh*	2	6	2	8	2	7
4. *Falsafah*	1	3	-	4	-	5
Languages						
5. Arabic	6	10	4	10	4	10
6. Malay	-	2	-	2	-	2
7. English	-	2	-	2	-	2
8. Social Studies	2	5	2	8	3	8
Total	17/15,13/15 (30)		14/12,16/18 (30)		14/13,16/17 (30)	

C. = Compulsory
E. = Elective
(Ministry of Education, Bangkok, Thailand, 1980/1982)

religious academic offerings of the Islamic private school must be upgraded and modeled on those of the Middle Eastern universities. Furthermore, the religious teachers (ustaz) must keep the academic standards of the Arabic-religious portion of their school system as high as those generally available in the more middle eastern countries. The higher that the standard of the Arabic-religious education in the Islamic private school becomes, the better the qualification value it maintains.

Scrutinizing the contents of the curriculum of Islamic studies offered in the public elementary schools and that of the Arabic-religious studies in the Islamic private schools, it is obvious that the Arabic language permeates the subject matter taught in the Islamic private schools, while the Thai language is much more prevalent in the subject matter provided in the public elementary schools. The reason behind this is clear. That is to say, the aim of teaching Islamic studies in public elementary schools is to convey the moral principles of Islam to Muslim children using the Thai language as the medium of instruction. Even though the Thai language is the medium in public schools, Arabic technical terms are found in every related subject, especially when in referring to the Quranic verses and the Prophetic traditions.

Examining the contents of the curriculum provided in the Islamic private school we find that all the textbooks are in Arabic and the Arabic language is used extensively as the medium of instruction.

When observing the Thai curriculum provided in the Islam private school, it is clear also that this school now offers a general Thai education equivalent to that of any government school.

Another important characteristic of the Islamic private school is the use of the Malay language. Besides the Malay subjects provided at the Ibtidâ'îyah (elementary level), Mutawassiṭah (middle level) and the Thânawîyah (secondary level), the Malay language also plays a necessary part in the programs a whole in its role as a means of interpreting the content of the Arabic texts.

From previous discussion of the Arabic-religious curricula used in the Islamic private school of Patani, it is clear that there are two different kinds of curricula. One is assigned by The Association of the Islamic Private Schools (Malay: Persatuan Sekolah Agama Rakyat, Arabic: Ittihâd al-Madâris al-Islâmîyah al-Ahlîyah), while the other is prescribed by the Office of Educational Region Two, Yala, and approved by the Thai Academic Department, Ministry of Education.

It is noteworthy that, although the Islamic institutions of Patani are under the guidance and supervision of the Office of Educational Region Two, there is still another type of independent Arabic school whose curriculum, method of teaching and textbooks are without government control. It is a modern type of school providing a range of subjects, mostly through the medium of the Arabic language. In downtown Patani, the Ma'had Dâr al-'Ulûm represents just such a school. This school offers only the al-Marḥalah al-Thânawîyah (the secondary level). It is, in fact, under the supervision of the Majlis Agama Islam Changwat Patani (The Patani Provincial Islamic Council). Most of the students who come to study at this school already have a good background in Arabic and Islam. Some of them have studied in the pondok for several years before joining the school to continue their studies. The regulations of the school require that, in order to sit in a particular class, the new students have to take a placement test for qualification.

This school also offers a special two-year program beyond the secondary level known as *qism al 'âlî,* which can result in the award of a diploma. In both secondary and diploma levels, imported Arabic books are used as the texts.

After meeting with a group of student studying at the secondary level, it is clear that they can function in the Arabic language so well that they can express their thoughts and feelings in Arabic clearly and fluently. On the other hand, the students of pondok schools often cannot express their ideas or their feelings in Arabic as fluently as the students of the Ma'had Dâr al-Ulûm and similar schools can. The students of the madrasah school of today generally speak Arabic as clearly as those of the Ma'had Dâr 'Ulûm, Patani.

One distinctive difference found in the pondok students is that they are very competent in reading the Arabic books in all the various subjects. They are capable of quoting the *matn* (content) of the texts easily and can refer to the branches of knowledge they learn while reading in a certain subject. This phenomenon cannot be found to the some degree in the madrasah students. This is almost certainly because the pondok students customarily learn subjects by rote.

Another distinctive feature of the Ma'had Dar al-Ulum is that no permanent ustaz (teachers) staff this school. Most of them take their turn in the teaching program as a voluntary duty to transmit the Arabic language and the message of Islam. During an interview with Ustaz Haji Ahmad Wan Lambut, the director of the Ma'had Dar al-Ulum, he related the historical background of the school. Ma'had Dar al-Ulum or Ma'had Samakum as it was first called, was established under the auspices of the Association of the Islamic private Schools of the four southern provinces by the end of 1970. By the end of 1974, the Association submitted this school to the supervision of the Patani Provincial Islamic Council. The subsequent inspection occurred in November 1975; since which time, the name of Ma'had Samakum was changed to Ma'had Dâr al-'Ulûm. This school is now recognized and accredited by the University of Riyadh, as well as the Islamic University, Medina, Kingdom of Saudi Arabia. The Ma'had Dâr al-'Ulûm is, in fact, a center of Arabic-religious learning, one that has inspired many young Muslims of Patani and the adjacent areas to obtain Islamic knowledge.

CHAPTER 7

The Government's Initiative and Response

Degree Programs at Prince of Songkla University

Conducting Arabic and Islamic studies programs and including the Arabic language in the university entrance exam as a foreign language subject.

Since the government launched the policy of educational reform in the pondok of the four southern provinces in 1970 the outcome of this reform becomes clear when one sees the students of the Islamic private school system being admitted directly to their courses of study at the university level in Thailand. Their ablity to study at the university level is due to their having obtained the higher secondary certificate of Thai education, provided in the Islamic private school, side-by-side with their Arabic-religious education. At the university level, these students have the option of choosing the areas of study that correspond with their desires. The students of the Islamic private school also have the opportunity to apply for the university places provided by the government for the Muslim students in the four southern provinces under the special quota system. This special quota (*quota phised* in Thai) has been in effect for a long time under the direction of the Ministry of the Interior to encourage Muslim students to attend a Thai University. Nantawan Haemindra makes a remark in the footnote of her article entitled "The Problem of the Thai-Muslims in the Four Southern Provinces of Thailand, Part 2," saying that fifty seats in the universities and in the Police Officer Cadet Academy have been reserved, since 1971, for Thai-Muslim students. A further sixteen scholarships have also been granted each year (Haemindra 1977). The students can apply to study in any university in Thailand. Under the project of the Ministry of the Interior, these students will be admitted to study at university level, provided that they pass the examination held among their Muslim peers from the four southern provinces, namely; Patani, Yala, Narathiwat and Satun. Another special quota is provided for the Muslim students from the five southern border provinces.

At this times, the Center for Coordination of Administration of the Southern Border Provinces, in Yala, South Thailand, is responsible for implementing the policy. The policy of this center is to promote education, not only for the Muslims in the four southern provinces mentioned above, but also the Muslims in Songkla province. This is because Songkla province was recently included under the umbrella of the southern border provinces of Thailand. Under the terms of this policy, these additional selected students can study only at Prince of Songkla University, but in any faculty in which they are interested, on the condition that they pass the exam. The policy provides for certain numbers of students based on the Muslim percentage in those provinces.

Recently, the policy of educational reform provided a special opportunity for Muslim students from the Islamic private schools. Those who obtain a higher secondary certificate of Thai education can join either the Islamic studies or Arabic program offered by the Faculty of Humanities and Social Sciences, Prince of Songkla University, Patani Campus, Thailand. These two programs are offered to any student who is qualified to follow the program designed by the Faculty.

The Islamic studies program is offered under the Department of Philosophy and Religion, while the Arabic program is offered under the Department of Thai and Oriental Languages, in the Faculty of Humanities and Social Sciences, Prince of Songkla University, Patani Campus. The Islamic studies program has been formally offered as a major subject since 1982.

In reply to the letter of the rector of Prince of Songkla University, asking to have the curriculum approved, Mr. Vichid Srisaan, the then deputy secretary to the Ministry of University Affairs, informed the rector about the matter in an official memorandum on January 9, 1981. The memorandum stated that the Ministry of Univerity Affairs had carefully considered the course structure for the degree of Bachelor of Arts, Islamic Studies, Faculty of Humanities and Social Sciences and given official approval on December 24, 1980. Later, the Office of the Civil Service Commission gave the degree accreditation on April 1981.

Prince of Songkla University follow the semester system in terms of the scheduling of its acedemic year. Each semester is approximately eighteen weeks in length. A summer term, which usually covers at least six weeks, is held in some years. Each credit at the university represents one hour of class time per week during the regular semester. Courses in the summer term meet more frequently to cover the same number of hours as class would take during a normal semester.

In accordance with the regulations of the Faculty of Humanities and Social Sciences, the first-year students, including those who want to take Islamic studies as their major, must take certain courses offered in liberal education. The major program of Islamic studies starts in the second year. The students who are majoring in Islamic studies must register for forty-eight credits in the major required courses and for at least three credits in the major elective courses.

Required Courses: Major Required Courses

Sixteen are offered, totaling 48 credits:

437-201 Basic Logic	(3)	Credits
439-211 Introduction to Islamic studies	(3)	"
439-214 Islam and Culture	(3)	"
439-319 The Prophetic Tradition 1	(3)	"
439-326 Islamic Law I	(3)	"
439-327 Economics in Islam	(3)	"
437-202 Ethics	(3)	"
439-212 Islamic Theology (*Tawhîd*)	(3)	"
349-215 Islamic History 1	(3)	"
439-320 Islamic Jurisprudence 1	(3)	"
439-325 Islam and Human Relations	(3)	"
437-203 Philosophy	(3)	"
439-213 Principles of Islam	(3)	"
439-318 The Holy Quran 1	(3)	"
439-323 Islamic Ethics	(3)	"
439-326 The Status of Muslim Women	(3)	"

Major Elective Courses

Students must choose from the following courses at least three credits.

427-214 Thai Society	(3)	Credits
439-216 Islamic History 2	(3)	"
439-322 Islamic Theology (*'Ilm al-Kalam*)	(3)	"
349-430 A Survey of Islamic Study	(3)	"
427-323 Research Theory in Social Sciences	(3)	"
437-417 Islamic Philosophy	(3)	"
439-328 Islamic Civilization	(3)	"
439-431 Comparative Religion	(3)	"
427-392 Muslim Society	(3)	"
439-321 The Source of Islamic Jurisprudence	(3)	"
439-429 Readings in Islamic Studies	(3)	"
439-432 The Role of Religion in Contemporary Society	(3)	"

Minor Courses

At present, the Faculty of Humanities and Social Sciences provides seventeen minor programs. Once a student chooses a major program offered in the Faculty, he or she must select a minor program whose courses are not offered in the major. The course credits required in the minor programs total between twenty to thirty-two. Additionally, the minor courses are structured in two groups: the minor required and the minor elective courses.

Minor in Thai Language and Literature

A student who chooses to study Thai language and literature as his or her minor must register for sixteen credits in the minor required courses and for at least eight credits in the minor elective courses. So, the complete program comprises twenty-four credits in total. The system of evaluation and grading must be the same as the regulations prescribe for those courses relating the language and literature major.

Minor in Chinese Language

A student who chooses Chinese language as a minor must register for twelve credits in the minor required courses and for at least eight credits in the minor elective courses.

Minor in Malay Language

A student who chooses Malay language as a minor must register for eleven credits in the minor required courses and for at least thirteen credits in the minor elective courses. For minor elective courses, students must choose from the major courses offered in the Malay language. The students are also permitted to select other courses offered in other departments, with the consultation and approval of both professors as well as heads of departments.

Minor in Arabic

A student who choose Arabic as a minor must register for fifteen credits in the minor required courses and for at least nine credits in the minor elective courses. In the minor elective courses, students are free to choose the courses from the major required and major elective courses offered in Arabic.

Minor in English Language

A student who wishes to take English language as a minor must register for twelve credits in the minor required courses and for at least twelve credits in minor elective courses. For the minor elective courses, it is required that the student choose from the courses that are offered to the major students, so as to complete the requirements of at least twenty-four credits in total.

Minor in English Language and Literature

A student choosing English language and literature as minor must register for nine credits in the minor required courses and for at least fifteen credits in the minor elective courses. For the minor elective courses, it is required that the student choose from the courses that are offered to the students majoring in English language and literature, so as to complete at least twenty-four credits in total.

Minor in French

A student choosing French as a minor must study 418-101 French 1 (3 credits) and 418-102 French 2 (3 credits), which offer basic instruction in the foreign language. Yet, these courses are not credited toward the minor. The student must take additional courses offered by the French division to the addition of at least twenty credits.

Minor in Library Science

A student taking library science as a minor must register for fiteen credits in the minor required courses and at least five credits in minor elective courses. The student should select the minor elective courses from the major elective courses offered.

Minor in History

A student taking history as a minor must register for 425-101 civilization (3 credits), which provides a general introduction to the Humanities. The student must register for six credits in the minor required courses and for at least eighteen credits in minor elective courses. It is recommended that the student choose selectives from the offerings of major elective and major required courses which are not the same as the minor required courses.

Minor in Geography

A student interested in geography as a minor must register for twelve credits in the minor required courses and at least nine credits in the minor elective courses of two areas. For the minor elective courses, the student is advised to select two areas from the major elective courses offered in the major program in geography.

Minor in Humanities and Social Studies

A student studying in this area must register for fourteen credits in the minor required courses and for at least eight credits in the minor elective courses. In the minor elective courses, the student is urged to select at least eight credits from the major elective courses offered in the major program of Humanities and Social Studies.

Minor in Social Development

A student taking the Social Development program as a minor must register for courses like 427-103 Introduction to Social Studies (2 credits) and 429-111 Introduction to Political Science (3 credits), whose credits are counted the same as they would be if they were elective courses. The student must earn eighteen credits in the minor required courses and no less than six credits in the minor elective courses to complete no less than twenty-four credits in total.

Minor in Political Science (Government)

A student studying in Political Science (Government) must register for eighteen credits in the minor required courses and for no less than nine credits in the minor elective courses. For the minor elective courses, the student is advised to choose from the major elective courses of the major program in Political Science, either in Plan A or Plan B, to gain at least nine credits.

Minor in American Studies

Students choosing American Studies as a minor must register for six credits in the minor required courses. they must also register for the minor elective courses, selecting from two or three fields. In each field at least six credits should be taken. The total credits should comprise at least twenty. The following courses are offered.

Field of History

425-429	General History of the U.S	(3)	Credits
430-311	Economic History of the U.S	(3)	"
430-312	Political History of the U.S	(3)	"
430-313	Intellectual History of the U.S	(3)	"
430-411	U.S and International Politics	(3)	"
430-412	Thai-U.S. Relations	(3)	"

Field of English Language

417-231	Grammer 1	(2)	"
417-232	Grammer 2	(2)	"
417-233	Writing 1	(2)	"
417-234	Writing 2	(2)	"
417-333	Writing 3	(2)	"
417-235	Basic Reading 1	(2)	"
417-236	Basic Reading 2	(2)	"

417-238	Listening-Speaking 1	(2)	"
417-239	Listening-Speaking 2	(2)	"
417-338	Listening-Speaking 3	(2)	"
417-435	Advanced Reading 1	(2)	"

Field of Geography

430-230	Geography of the U.S	(3)	"
430-231	Historical Geography of the U.S	(3)	"
430-330	Resources and the Problem of Their Use by the U.S	(3)	"
430-331	Land Use in the U.S	(3)	"
430-430	Economic Geography of the U.S	(3)	"
430-431	Social Geography of the U.S	(3)	"

Field of Political Science

429-111	Introduction to Political Science	(3)	"
429-316	Politics-Government of the U.S	(3)	"
430-241	Systems of the U.S	(3)	"
430-340	Elections and Political Parties of the U.S	(3)	"
430-341	Presidential Institution of the U.S	(3)	"
430-440	International Policy of the U.S	(3)	"
430-441	Seminar: Comparative Politics between U.S and Thailand	(3)	"

Field of American Literature

430-251	American Literature in Thai Translation	(3)	"
430-350	Cultural Processes in American Society	(3)	"
430-351	General Reading	(3)	"
430-352	American Drama	(3)	"
417-421	American Poetry	(3)	"
417-423	American Novel	(3)	"
417-429	Advanced Studies in American Literature	(3)	"
430-450	Selected American Writers	(3)	"

Field of Social Sciences

427-103	Introduction to Social Sciences	(3)	"
430-260	American Culture	(3)	"
430-261	Social Structure of the U.S	(3)	"
430-360	Institution of the American Family	(3)	"
430-361	Social Problems of the U.S	(3)	"
430-460	Problems of Population of the U.S	(3)	"
430-461	Social Change in American Society	(3)	"

Minor in Philosophy

A student studying in philosophy as a minor must register for nine credits in the minor required courses and for at least eleven credits in the minor elective courses. In the minor elective, the student may choose either from the major required or elective courses in the major program of philosophy, which have a value of at least eleven credits.

Minor in Religion

A student choosing to study in religion as a minor must register for nine credits in the minor required courses and for at least eleven credits in the minor elective courses.

Minor in Islamic Studies

A student who is interested in Islamic as a minor must register for twenty-four credits in the minor required courses and at least six credits in the minor elective courses.

The above descriptions are the details of the course areas covered by the minor programs offered by the Faculty of Humanities and Social Sciences, Prince of Songkla University. The Muslim students who are studying in the Islamic Studies Program must choose any one of these areas to broaden their education. It is hoped that the scope of these course offerings will be further broadened. The career opportunities of the Islamic studies students will be greater if they are allowed to take a second major offered in the Faculty. This can be achieved only if the current educational policy at Prince of Songkla University is reconsidered. As result of such a change it is believed, that the intellectual awareness of the Muslim students would become broader.

Concerning the Arabic program offered at the Faculty of Humanities and Social Sciences, it is clear that the government has moved another step forward in developing meaningful plans to cope with the need of the Muslim people of Thailand. In this case, Prince of Songkla University fills a significant function in providing the Arabic program in the upper level of undergraduate studies, particularly for those who come from the Islamic private school. In the discussion which follows I will provide more details about the Arabic program and its curriculum as well as its prospects.

The rationale and objective of having Arabic offered as a major subject are clearly stated. The Faculty of Humanities and Social Sciences, Prince of Songkla University aims primarily at teaching Arabic in order to create an atmosphere of mutual understanding among the people of different cultural backgrounds in the multiethnic society that is Thailands. In addition to that, the Arabic language is considered to be an important language of the world today.

It was clearly mentioned in the Higher Educational Development Plan, the Fifth Plan (1982-1986), that the Arabic language is considered to be a very important subject which, at that time, Prince of Songkla University had already included in its prospectus as an elective course offered in liberal education by the Faculty of Humanities and Social Sciences. Furthermore, the Faculty had already prepared to offer Arabic as a major program. Thereafter, the project was submitted to the Ministry of University Affairs in order to have Arabic officially offered as a major program for the degree of Bachelor of Arts.

According to the official document signed by Mr. Kamhaeng Sathirakul, Deputy to the Under-Secretary of the Ministry of University Affairs, dated October 6, 1986, in reply to the rector of Prince of Songkla University concerning the proposal addressed to Ministry of University Affairs, the Arabic curriculum for the Bachelor of Arts was accredited. This meant that the Ministry of University Affairs had approved the Arabic curriculum. This approval was then forwarded to the Office of the Civil Service Commission of Thailand. Therefore the program was here after being certified. The objectives of this program still are:

1. To offer a degree program (B.A) in Arabic and to prepare students with a high degree of competence in this chosen field.
2. To promote study and research in Arabic in a wider scope.
3. To provide academic services to the interested persons especially teachers and students studying Arabic.
4. To support and cooperate with the College of Islamic Studies at Prince of Songkla University in the academic field and the major program of Islamic studies as well.

The above objectives are clearly written in the new Arabic curriculum prospects of the year 1986. The objectives show that the Arabic language has assumed a place of importance not only in the private sectors but also in the governmental units. They also indicate that the Arabic language offered in the University is aimed at promoting it as well as offering service to those who are interested in acquiring the knowledge. This implies that the Arabic program offered by the Faculty of Humanities and Social Sciences, Prince of Songkla University, has been designed to serve the need of people in Thailand as a whole and the Muslim community in particular. It is confirmed that, throughout the history of higher education in Thailand, the Arabic language has never before been introduced into academic circles. Thus, the program offered at Prince of Songkla University is considered the first of its kind ever to exist in the academic arena of Thailand. This academic significance should be attributed to the efforts of the administrators of Prince of Songkla University who were farsighted in supporting the establishment of an Arabic program at the University. The Arabic program, in fact, has emerged on the scene to bring the light of new knowledge to the people of Thailand. This light illuminates the good intentions of the Thai government, for it provides a new field of study for the Thai people.

The Arabic program provided in the Faculty of Humanities and Social Sciences is set up on two lines, i.e., the major and the minor. It is also provided as an elective subject for the students who need to study Arabic for their daily usage and to access reading materials or, for business purposes. It is not surprising that most of those students who take Arabic as their major are the students from the Islamic private school. This new educational opportunity reflects the initiative of the governmental sector in responding to the needs of the Muslim people in Thailand as a whole and in the southern border provinces in particular. With the establishment of the Arabic degree program in the Faculty of Humanities and Social Sciences, the government also expects that the University can at the very least solve the problem of Muslim students going to study in Middle Eastern countries. However, the fact is that, although the government has established the Arabic program in the University, the sending of Muslim children to study abroad continues. Indeed, it increases in numbers every year and it is still true that, a number of those desirous to have university education will go abroad to Cairo as well as to Mecca, (not to mention other Middle Eastern countries) either on scholarship or at their own expenses (Haemindra 1977). This is because many Muslim countries nowadays provide annual scholarships to the Muslim students throughout Thailand; either through the private sector or government channels. This is one important reason. Another reason is that the Arabic program at Prince of Songkla University admits a small number of students and provides a small number of seats. The limited number of seats cannot cover the actual numbers of the Muslim students, requiring places particularly those from the Islamic private schools.

The chances for the Muslim students to study the Arabic program in Thailand must be increased and more seats should be provided. The very limited number of students joining the Arabic program at Prince of Songkla University can been seen in Table 7.1.

To make the Arabic program more effective, the University plans to appoint more Arabic lecturers to meet its own resource needs. Table 7.2 shows the number of Arabic lecturers that are required to be added to the teaching staff during the academic years 1986-90. This is the very first step of the expansion program. Another of the important keys to keeping the program at this University successful are farsighted authorities and administrators who can bring its academic goals to full fruition.

TABLE 7.1 Number of students studying Arabic as their major
and minor during the first five-year period

Academic Year	1986		1987		1988		1989		1990	
Number of students	Mj. *	Mn. *	Mj.	Mn.	Mj.	Mn.	Mj.	Mn.	Mj.	Mn.
First year**	-	-	-	-	-	-	-	-	-	-
Second year	-	10	10	10	10	10	10	20	10	20
Third year	-	-	-	10	10	10	10	10	10	20
Fourth year	-	-	-	-	-	10	10	10	10	10
Total		10	10	20	20	30	30	40	30	50
Expected graduates	-	-	-	-	-	-	10	10	10	10

* Mj., Mn. = Major and Minor
** = Students are not yet allowed to choose their major
Source: New Arabic Curriculum & Prospectus, Faculty of Humanities and Social
Sciences, Prince of Songkla University, Patani, Thailand, 1986.

TABLE 7.2 The recruitment plan of Arabic lecturers
in the Arabic program at the university

Years	1986	1987	1988	1989	1990	Total
Degree and area of study	M.A Arabic lang.	B.A Arabic lang./ lit.	B.A Arabic lang./ lit.	M.A Arabic lit.	M.A Arabic lang./ lit.	
Number	1	1	1	1	1	5

Source: New Arabic Curriculum Prospectus, Faculty of Humanities and Social
Sciences, Prince of Songkla University, Patani, Thailand 1986

The Arabic program at Prince of Songkla University, stands alone as the
only high-level academic program as its kind for the young generation
throughout Thailand. It appears to serve the intellectual purposes that link
the University to the outside world. The real obligation of the University
program is to find every possible way to enrol more students from the Islamic
private schools from all over Thailand so that they will have a chance to
study in a national institution.

The Arabic courses offered in the Faculty of Humanities and Social Sciences, Prince of Songkla University are listed below. It is required that a student majoring in Arabic complete the major required and elective courses for at least fifty-five credits in total.

The major required courses are forty-one credits

They are as follows:

414-111	Introduction to Arabic	(3)	Credits
414-211	Structure of Arabic 1	(3)	"
414-212	Structure of Arabic 2	(3)	"
414-216	Structure of Arabic 3	(3)	"
414-221	Listening-Speaking in Arabic 1	(2)	"
414-227	Reading in Arabic 1	(2)	"
414-228	Reading in Arabic 2	(2)	"
414-255	Introduction to History of Arabic Lit.	(3)	"
414-320	Practical Phonetics	(3)	"
414-322	Listening-Speaking 2	(2)	"
414-323	Listening-Speaking 3	(2)	"
414-324	Listening-Speaking 4	(2)	"
414-329	Reading in Arabic 3	(2)	"
414-332	Arabic Writing 1	(2)	"
414-333	Arabic Writing 2	(2)	"
414-357	Appreciation of Arabic Literature	(3)	"
414-434	Arabic Writing 3	(2)	"

It is required to take at least fourteen credits from the major elective courses

The courses offered are:

414-325	Listening-Speaking 5	(2)	"
414-330	Reading in Arabic 4	(2)	"
414-339	Arabic Speech	(3)	"
414-351	Arabic Literature 1	(2)	"
414-352	Arabic Literature 2	(2)	"
414-361	Arabic Culture	(3)	"
414-363	Arabic for Tourism 1	(2)	"
414-364	Arabic for Tourism 2	(2)	"
414-314	Arabic Structure 4	(3)	"
414-317	Arabic Structure 5	(3)	"
414-435	Arabic Writing 4	(2)	"
414-438	Translation 1	(2)	"
414-438	Translation 2	(2)	"
414-440	Arabic Workshop	(2)	"
414-442	Law and Its Terminology in the Arab Countries	(2)	"

According to the curriculum structure outlined by the Faculty of Humanities and Social Sciences, Prince of Songkla University, there are regulations concerning the courses and credits students have to take. They are as follows:

1. The liberal education course required   (41) Credits
2. Major course required   (50-62)   "
3. Minor courses required   (20-32)   "
4. Elective courses required   (6-32)   "

Considering the need to provide education for the Muslim students at the higher level, the administrators and the educators of Prince of Songkla University have launced the policy of promoting education to the young Muslims of the South. As a national educational centre, Prince of Songkla University has conducted a direct entrance examination for higher secondary students who have been schooled in the fourteen provinces of southern Thailand. The policy of conducting this direct examination is to get more students from the southern part of Thailand to study in their nearest institution, located in the south. For this reason and others, Prince of Songkla University has provided this special opportunity, directed mainly at the students of the Islamic private school.

The University suggest that those who obtain a higher secondary certificate of Thai education with Arabic-religious background take Arabic as a foreign language instead of French for the University Entrace Exam. In order to enroll in the University, they have to pass subjects like Thai, Social Studies and English. These students who take Arabic as their foreign language and pass their examination can select either the Islamic studies or the Arabic program as their major field. For the minor program they have the option to pick any field they are interested in. This project is considered the first of its kind ever conducted at the university level. It began in 1982 and continue up to the present time.

The entrance examinations for Arabic evaluate how well the Muslim students have mastered Arabic and assess their capacity to follow the Arabic major and the Islamic studies program. It contains several sections; such as *al-uslûb wa-al-ta'bîr* (Arabic style and expression), *adab wa-nuṣûṣ* (Arabic literature), *muṭâla'ah* (reading comprehension) and *naḥw wa-ṣarf* (grammar and morphology). Most of the materials are taken from the curriculum and textbooks taught in the Islamic private school. The questions are given in multiple choice form. Prior to the University Entrance Examination every year, Prince of Songkla University appoints certain persons to have direct contact with the administrators of Islamic private schools in southern Thailand in order to inform them about the policy of Prince of Songkla University with regard to the Muslim students. Sometimes, the University arranges a special meeting in the University campus, inviting the Administrators of the Islamic private schools, in which Thai education reaches the level of a high secondary certificate, to discuss the educational issues that might benefit the Muslim students of southern Thailand as a whole.

Establishing the College of Islamic Studies

The existing Islamic studies program at the University was still considered a small unit. It was run under the Department of Philosophy and Religion and could not fully serve the needs of the people to the extent expected of a government university. The administrators of Prince of Songkla University studied the significance and the advantages of providing Islamic education on a wider scale. They concluded that Islamic education at the university level should cover a full program of study. To meet the needs of the people and to realize the government's desire to see its Muslim students attend Thai universities, the University proposed to establish a College of Islamic Studies, as an independent faculty, to provide an academic program and research opportunities. The original idea of establishing this college was put forward in 1982, but its founding concept goes back to early 1974 (Baka nd.) during which an academic exhibition on Patani campus entitled "Local Cultural Art of the South," was held.

Prince of Songkla University outlined the purposes of the establishment, which were to support the cultural background of the Muslim people living in the southern border provinces of Thailand. There are many sensitive, complicated problems in the four southern border provinces of Thailand when compared to other regions in the country. These complicated problems, whether socio-economic or political, must be sincerely faced. To provide good education and to help serve the education real needs of the people are important factors contributing toward nation building. To serve these ends, the College of Islamic Studies outlined its objectives as follows:

1. To serve the interest of the national security policy.
2. To serve the unity and integrity of the nation.
3. To create mutual understanding and cooperation among communities.
4. To serve as a center of Islamic education.
5. To develop the ethics and moral standards of the people so that they become an asset to their society and to others.
6. To abide by the Quran as the guideline of the College.

There is a long historical background to the College of Islamic Studies project. The momentum that encouraged the government to have such a College built at Prince of Songkla University was derived from efforts to solve the problems of the southern border provinces, an area which had for so long been the focus of government concern. Due to these important considerations, the National Security Council outlined its objectives and goals and made a proposal to the Cabinet. On January 24, 1978, the Cabinet approved the objectives proposed by the National Security Council. In line with the national development process; the national Economic and Social Plan, the Fifth Plan (1982-1986) had included the establishment of an Islamic center at Prince of Songkla University. The objective of this center was to provide Islamic education up to university level. The project was discussed in detail among the administrators.

The drafting committee of the project also discussed the College's potential to serve the needs of the government concerning solving the problems in the Southern border provinces of Thailand. As a result, during the third meeting held on May 31, 1984, they first submitted to the Patani campus committee, a proposal that would establish an Institute of Islamic Studies. Later on, the ninth session of the deans, held on July 17, 1984, approved the proposal and suggested that the proposal be submitted to the University Council and to the Ministry of University Affairs for their collective deliberations.

The process of establishing the College of Islamic Studies at Prince of Songkla University, in fact, has been through several phases and with different designations such as "Center" and "Institution". The outlines of each phase can be seen as:

1. *First Phase: Proposal of the Project* (January-September 1984)
    a. Drafting the College of Islamic Studies Project.
    b. Submitting the project to the University in order to get approval from the University Council of Prince of Songkla University, as well as from the committee of the Ministry of University Affairs.
    c. Requesting quotas and budgets.

2. *Second Phase: Establishment and Preparation* (October 1984 - September 1986)
    a. The process of preparing personnel.
    b. The process of preparing buildings and equipment.
    c. The process of providing community services, research, in-service training and seminars up to the end of the National Economic and Social Development Plan, The Fifth Plan (1982-86).
    d. The process of finding academic aid, to develop the College, from the Middle Eastern countries and others.
    e. The planning process of the College during the National Economic and Social Development Plan, Sixth Plan (1987-91).

3. *Third Phase: The completion of the Process* (1987-91)
    a. The process of seeking approval of the curricula for the associate degree, baccalaureate degree, master's degree and doctoral degree in Islamic Studies from the Ministry of University Affairs and the Office of the Civil Service Commision.
    b. The process of transferring the Islamic studies program from the Faculty of Humanities and Social Sciences to the College of Islamic Studies.
    c. The process of educating personnel for various types of posts.
    d. The process of preparing college students who will enter Islamic Studies.
    e. The process of research and giving academic service to the community during the National Economic and Social Development Plan, Sixth Plan.

The College of Islamic Studies has planned to launch an intensive training program in Islam for government officials in the southern border provinces. To accomplish this goal the College cooperated with the Center for Coordination of Administration of the Southern Border Provinces in Yala, and other governmental offices. A short program leading to a certificate also will be provided for the graduates who have finished high secondary level. This certificate will qualify them to teach in elementary schools. Furthermore, the College of Islamic Studies will offer a two-year certificate program in Arabic and Islamic Studies to the students who have completed their study at al-thânawîyah level and obtained the secondary certificate of Thai education. This will qualify them to teach in high schools.

In the degree program, the College of Islamic studies will handle the undergraduate students of Islamic Studies from the Faculty of Humanities and Social Sciences, as soon as the process of transformation is completed. The master's degree program will be offered in *Sharî'ah* (Islamic Law), *Usûl al-Dîn* (Theology), *Da'wah* (Propagation of Faith), *Ta'rîkh wa-Hadârah* (History and Civilization). If the personnel and staff of the College are strong enough and ready to serve a complete academic program, the doctoral program may be offered during the National Economic and Social Development Plan, the Seventh Plan (1992-1996). In order to make the administrative process accord with the policy of the National Security Council concerning the southern border provinces and to cope with the major burdens of the University, the College of Islamic Studies assigns its administrative responsibilities to offices and personnel as shown in Figure 7.1.

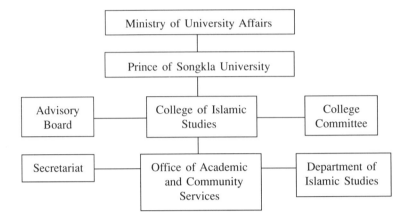

FIGURE 7.1   The Administration System and Organization of the College of
Islamic Studies at Prince of Songkla University

During the period of preparation, the College of Islamic Studies conducted several academic seminar, both internal and external.   The first
seminar, entitled "Seminar for Establishment of the Islamic Center," was held
on 27-29 May 1983.   At this meeting, there were forty-two participants and
twenty-three observers.   The major aims of this seminar were outlined as:

1. The respond to the goal and policy of the government in accordance with
   the national Economic and Social Development Plan, Fifth Plan (1982-86)
2. To abide by Islamic rules as a philosophical guidance in establishing the
   Islamic Center.
3. To accumulate opinions and ideas from intellectuals of various sectors
   pertaining to the establishment of the Islamic Center.
4. To find concrete concepts and ideas for the Islamic Center.
5. To find the most practical way to respond to the regional need of (and
   for) Islamic Studies.
6. To study and prepare for the international seminar.

After this seminar, the administrators of Prince of Songkla University
were convinced that a College of Islamic Studies must be established in
Patani.   As the ancient center of Malay Muslim education, Patani is a
promising site for replanting the seeds of the Islamic intellectual heritage.

The second, actually a product of the first, was held on July 20-22, 1985.
The title of the seminar was "Islam: The Way of Life."   Seventy-nine
participants and more than thirty-three observers attended, coming from
various parts of southern Thailand, including Songkla, Pattalung, Nakorn Si
Thammaraj, Trang, Surat Thani and Pangnga. There were also a few partici-

pants from Central Bangkok. Among the guest speakers were Mohammad bin Haji Abdul Majid and Ramli bin Haji Abdullah. Both are lecturers at the University of Malaya, Nilam Puri Campus, Kelantan, Malaysia. This was clear indication that the staff of the Islamic Studies project had begun to have direct contact with scholars outside Thailand. It was a step towards creating an academic liaison with other institutions on the international level. To help the discussion advance most effectively and efficiently, the Thai and Malay languages were both used throughout the meeting. It is politic to mention here that the U.S. - based Asia Foundation funded both seminars.

The idea of having the College of Islamic Studies at Prince of Songkla University introduced to the world outside began when Mr. Mohammad Tawfiq Uwaida, then Secretary-General of the Supreme Council for Islamic Affairs, Cairo, Egypt, accompanied by Professor Mohsin Abd Al-Rahman Abu Sida of the Faculty of Languages and Translation, al-Azhar University, Cairo, Egypt, visited Prince of Songkla University in 1974. Mr. 'Uwaida had an opportunity to discuss with Dr. Sawad Sakulthai, then Rector of Prince of Songkla University and the university staff, the possibility of establishing the Arabic and Islamic Studies program at the university and its potential future. As a result of this visit and the resulting discussions, the Egyptian government officially invited a delegation from Prince of Songkla University to visit Cairo, Egypt, to engage in a study tour. The delegation was headed by Dr. Chamnarn Prathomsinth and accompanied by two lecturers, Ananta O'Krissa and Hassan Madmarn. This took place in November 18-29, 1974.

Initially, the Egyptian government donated ten thousand pounds towards the development of the teaching of Arabic and Islamic Studies program. (Nation (Bangkok) Oct. 31 1974) . Later in the same year, Shaykh Hasan al-Tohamy, then secretary-general of the Islamic Secretariat, Jeddah, paid a visit to the southern border provinces of Thailand, where he conferred with the governors and the authorities of Prince of Songkla University, Patani. This happened after the 1974 conference of Islamic foreign ministers, held in Kuala Lumpur, Malaysia (Suhrke & Noble 1977). Subsequently, on April 13, 1984 Dr. Seddik Taouti, Assistant President of the Islamic Development Bank (IDB), Jeddah, made an official visit to Prince of Songkla University. Dr. Taouti was interested in the project of a College of Islamic Studies. He agreed to support the project and required that the University submit a complete, detailed proposal.

In July 1985, the president of the International Islamic Charitable Fund, Kuwait, Shaykh Yusuf al-Hajj, accompanied by Hashim Non-Anant, the manager of The Islamic Foundation of Ansarussunah, Pakpayoon, Patthalung Province, paid a visit to Prince of Songkla University. During the meeting, Shaykh Yusuf al-Hajj attended a briefing on the College of Islamic Studies, given by Acharn Pann Yuanlaie, Vice Rector of Prince of Songkla University

Patani Campus. Shaykh Yusuf was interested in the project and hoped to give material support, provided that the project was well-run.

Tunku Abdul Rahman, the ex-Prime Minister of Malaysia, expressed his gratitude to the Thai government for having an Islamic Studies Center established at Prince of Songkla University. As the president of the Regional Islamic Da'wah Council of Southeast Asia and the Pacific (RISEAP), Tunku told the participants at their second general assembly held in Kuala Lumpur in June 4-5, 1983, that he was ready to support the project and find charitable funds for the purpose (Matichon Bangkok Oct. 11. 1988).

Thus, from the seminar discussion and the exchange of ideas among the administrators and the government authorities, as well as from the visits of very important persons from the Muslim countries, came a clear notion of how to make the College of Islamic Studies project possible. Moreover, the committee for the establishment of the college and the administrators of Prince of Songkla University continued to labor for project approval by the Ministry of University Affairs and the Cabinet.

The dream of having a College of Islamic Studies built at Prince of Songkla University came true when the National Security Council proposes the project to the Cabinet for approval. Eventually, on October 11, 1988, the project was officially put before the cabinet. It was suggested that this project would bring dignity and pride to the Muslims of Thailand as a whole. *Matichon*, a leading newspaper in Bangkok, gave further details about the process, saying that the Secretary-General to the National Security Council, Mr. Suwit Suththanukul, had proposed the project of establishing the College of Islamic Studies at Prince of Songkla University to the Prime Minister, Chatchâi Chonhawan. Mr. Suththanukul had done so in order to get permission to allow Prince of Songkla University to develop the Islamic Studies program, as it was then moved from the Philosophy and Religion Department, to become a college which would have equal status with the other faculties in the university. It is reported that the project was proposed to the Cabinet on October 11, 1988 (Siamrat (Bangkok) June 8, 1983).

With the establishing of this college at Prince of Songkla University, the National Security Council hoped primarily to solve the educational problems of the southernmost provinces. The Ministry of Foreign Affairs and the Fourth Army Area as well as the Center for Coordination of Administration of the Southern Border Provinces in Yala must continue to cooperate with each other, working hand in hand in order to implement the government's policies. The report also said that the development of the college would, at least, accomplish three things: (1) block the interference of foreign countries in supporting the students to study abroad, (2) meet the community needs, and (3) help Prince of Songkla University to become an academic center of education, research, community and personnel development, both for governmental units and the private sector. As a center of research, it would explore ideas for the benefit of the society in various fields.

Taking an optimistic view, the College of Islamic Studies project must be approved by the Cabinet, for the objectives of the college are clearly outlined. They indicate that the college would help serve not only academic purposes, but also the national security policies in various ways.

Though the government seeks to open a door of opportunity to the students from the Islamic private schools to enrol in Arabic and Islamic Studies programs at Prince of Songkla University, the Muslim elites of southern Thailand continue to think of having a private institution established to serve their children, especially those from the Islamic private schools. The first such private institution of its kind is actually already established in Yala, under the supervision of Haji Ahmad Husayn, the former Muslim judge (Malay-Arabic: Tok Qâdi) of Yala. This institution, which is called in Arabic, Kullîyat Mu'allimîn (Teachers College), is aimed at training teachers who will teach Arabic to non-native speakers. It is expected that most of its graduates will teach in the Islamic private schools of the four southern provinces of Thailand. The college project has taken Phattana Vitya School, Yala, south Thailand, as the site of its temporary headquarters and administration. The budget has been initially funded by the Islamic Development Bank (IDB), Jeddah with the approval of Dr. Seddik Taouti, the assistant president of the Bank. On January 1, 1988, for the ceremony of the laying of the 'cornerstone', Dr. Taouti was invited to take part as representative of the Islamic Development Bank. The ceremony was attended by more than two hundred distinguished guests.

Besides the project of training instructors in the teaching of Arabic to non-native speakers, provided by the Teachers College mentioned above, there is another project that carries the name of the Islamic College of South Thailand. This project is called in Arabic, al-Kullîyah al-Islâmîyah Janûb Thailand. The initiative for the project started when a group of Muslim students from Patani gathered (probably at King Saud University in Riyadh) to discuss the future of the Muslim students from the Islamic private schools who finish their higher secondary certificate of Thai and Arabic-religious education. The discussion led to several other meetings being held among the Muslim students from Patani. As a result, the complete proposal was made to have the issue discussed with those who are concerned in the matter, especially the World Assembly of Muslim Youth (WAMY). They named the proposal, Project of Establishment of an Islamic College of South Thailand. It has been strongly supported by the Muslim elites of Thailand in general and of Patani in particular. During the two meetings of the project committee which were held August 6-7, 1987, at the Mu'assasah al-Thaqâfah al-Islâmîyah (the Foundation for Islamic Education) site of their temporary office, 867 Siroros Road, Yala, I met several Muslim leaders whose functions are to support the Arabic and Islamic Studies programs in the Islamic private schools.

I also discussed with several dignitaries their views on how the project to establish an Islamic College of South Thailand could be brought about. According to statements made by Dr.'Abd al-Khâliq al-Qudsî, a representative of WAMY, an Islamic College of South Thailand will receive strong support from the world outside, especially from WAMY itself. This is confirmed by an official letter written by the Assistant Secretary-General of WAMY, Dr. Ibrahim Hamd al-Qa'id. In reply to a letter from Hassan 'Abd al-Qâdir, the chairman of the project, dated 18 Jumâda 2nd, 1407 A.H., 1987, Dr. Hamd al-Qa'îd expresses a wish to see official approval from the Thai government so that the formalities for material support can be accelerated (Hamd to Abd al-Qâdir 1987). The project seems to be running smoothly as far as the manner in which the proposed concept has been received internationally, but what seems to be a solid and impregnable wall to break through is the Thai government's attitude towards a project of this nature and magnitude. To the best of my knowledge, the project is supported by high-ranking officials and officers of Thailand in order to get the approval from the government. However, up to this moment, there are no further accessible details about this project. It is important to remark that this college, if it were approved, would provide modern academic education such as business, computer science, social sciences, Arabic and Islamic studies. All these branches of study would be essentially based on Islam as the moral and philosophical foundation of thought.

The educational movements of the Muslim elites of southern Thailand describe above reflect, more or less, a perceived need for educational reform in this region. They look at the future of the education of the Muslim children beyond the Islamic private schools as a significant problem that must be carefully solved. Such private institution, in fact, can serve as additional educational support for the national education reform policy in the truest sense.

CHAPTER 8

Conclusion

Islamic education in the Muslim community of Patani, Southern Thailand, and the nearby areas preserves, up to the present time, certain characteristics in keeping with the intellectual traditions of the past. The pondok, the traditional school of the Muslims of Patani, has provided Islamic education to the Muslim, not only in Patani, but also in Thailand as a whole. Furthermore, this institution served in the past as a center of Islamic traditional learning for the Muslims of Cambodia, Malaysia and Indonesia as well. Patani, in fact, used to occupy a place of honor in the transmission of traditional Islamic learning to the Malay-Muslim world.

Patani, whose majority population was originally Malay Muslims, speaking Malay in their daily lives, yet designated Thai citizens, became well-known, not only because of its prominence in history as a center of Islam, but also because of the widely-acclaimed ulama who lived and wrote there. In fact, the works of the ulama of Patani of those past generations are still being read and used in all circles, ranging from groups of common folk up to the *alim ulama* (A Malay expression meaning "Muslim scholars") of the Malay-Muslim world. For the ordinary Muslim citizens, or for students at the lower levels, the works of the Patani ulama which are known as Kitab Jawi, serve as the basic foundation for learning about Islam. The Malay language used in the Kitab Jawi, frequently refered to as the Lisan al-Jawi, is the language spoken by most of the people in the Malay Peninsula, including the Patani region. Besides the Kitab Jawi, several major Arabic books are also read in the pondok. Those who want to seek Islamic knowledge in depth usually stay in the pondok for several years, studying under chosen tok guru for specialization in a certain field.

The Patani ulama wrote Kitab Jawi in order to teach their fellow countrymen, for most of the Malays do not know much Arabic. These Kitab Jâwî serve not only the Malay Muslims living in the communities of Southeast Asia, but also those domiciled either permanently or temporarily in the Holy City, Mecca. These Malays living in Mecca usually study under particular ulama from Patani and Indonesia.

Among those ulama of the first generation serving their fellow countrymen in Mecca were Shaykh Dawud al-Fatani and Shaykh Ahmad al-Fatani. The second generation were Pak Do 'Ae Mahla (Ismail bin Shaykh Abd al-Qadir Bendang Daya, Patani) and Pak Do 'Ae Semla (Ismail bin Haji Wan Ahmad, Tok Semla Tua, Patani) as well as Shaykh Godir (Abd al-Qadir) al-Mandilî of Indonesia. At the present time, Kru Sen (Haji Husayn Surat and

Kru Li (Haji Ali) Chaiya are the two Muslim scholars from Thailand teaching in Masjid al-Haram. They are considered to be the third generation teaching their fellow countrymen in this holy place. The Muslims of Thailand in Mecca usually acquire an advanced knowledge of the Islamic intellectual disciplines under the roof of Masjid al-Haram, though they sometimes go individually to read certain Kitab at the houses of their Patani Malay mentors.

A significant part of the Jawi Islamic literature known as the Kitab Jawi are the works of the ulama of Patani. Most of these treatises were compiled, written or translated when their authors were in Mecca. They wrote mostly in Jawi, the classical Malay language. This use of Jawi becomes one of the most significant characteristics of the Islamic literature of the Malay Muslim community. This is because the Kitab Jawi stand firmly as the major foundation of Islamic education process enabling the seekers of knowledge to dig into the Islamic precept in depth. The well-known works of Jâwî Islamic literature owe their reputation to the basic importance of their contents and their usefulness in providing Islamic intellectual learning to those who need it.

The major goal of the Patani ulama in writing Kitab Jawi in Malay was to help the Malay Muslim community, whose mother tongue is Malay, to understand Islamic thought. However, through written or oral translation into Thai, they reach the Thai-speaking group of the Muslim community in Thailand as well.

Besides being intimately bound to the history of the communities in the Malay Muslim World, the Kitab Jawi of the Patani ulama also link their readers with the scholarly world of Middle Eastern countries and especially Mecca and Cairo. In Mecca, the Kitab Jawi are considered to be an important part of Islamic literature, alongside Turkish and Arabic works. For some years after 1884, their printing received special attention from the printing presses of Mecca. In Cairo, they were accorded a respect equal in degree to that of Mecca. Most of the major Kitab Jawi written by the ulama of Patani were printed with particular care at a Cairo press under the editorial super-vision of some of the ulama of al-Azhar. From the 'Isá al-Bâbî al-Halabî press in Cairo, most of the Kitab Jawi were produced and distributed to the Malay Muslim world of Southeast Asia. As suitable printing facilities became available closer to home, the printing of Kitab Jawi was gradually taken over by the Sulaymân Mar'i Press in Singapore. Later, the Maktabat wa-Matba'at Dar al-Maarif Press in Penang, Malaysia, took full responsibility for produc-ing the major Kitab Jawi of the Patani ulama, especially when the Sulaymân Mar'î Press ceased to function. Since then, the Maktabat wa-Matba'at Dar al-Maarif, Penang, Malaysia, has become the backbone of publishing for the Kitab Jawi. This printing press belongs to Muhammad Nahdî whose permanent home has been Patani since he emigrated there from Hadramawt. In fact, the Kitab Jawi of the Patani ulama have played the most substantial role in connecting the Mecca scholarly authorities and the Cairo printing presses to the Muslim community of Patani, from past decades to the present day.

In the downtown area of Patani, there are also three Malay-owned printing houses that serve mainly to publish the Malay Islamic literature of the Patani ulama of the past and of the tok gurus as well as of the ustaz. Through these printing presses, the Malay Islamic literature of Patani survives. The survival of the Kitab Jawi, of course, means much more for the Muslim community at large. The community needs to realize more fully the critical role of the owners of those printing presses. Their endeavor in maintaining the Jawi Islamic literature is indeed commendable.

During the recent process of educational reform and change, the pondok institution, before transforming its structure into the Islamic private school, first changes its organization into a form loosely patterned after the modern madrasah of the Arab countries. The tendency to transform the pondok into the madrasah started in 1970 when the government launched a policy of educational reform throughout the country. With this education reform policy, the tok gurus realized that the policy of the government would directly and indirectly touch and influence the essence of traditional Islamic education in the pondok. Fearing that the policy would undermine the whole apparatus of traditional Islamic education the tok gurus then felt compelled to bring the purposes and curriculum of the pondok into the madrasah system, though they were not yet really prepared for it. Assuming a watchful attitude, the tok gurus hoped to bring more modern methods of teaching and learning into the pondok and in the meantime to maintain its traditional curriculum, guarding the institution against the perils of modernist education reform.

To handle this situation, the tok gurus send their children to study in the Muslim countries, including those of the Middle East. They hope that their own children will be properly oriented toward Arabic and Islamic education. It turn, they can manage the new system of education in the pondok as soon as they return home. These young graduates have however, subtly adjusted the methods of the pondok to bring them into line with the educational system of the madrasah as found in Arab Muslim countries. With the efforts of the tok gurus and the energy and ideas of the young graduates, the madrasah system of Patani, whose curriculum and syllabus are conducted under the Ittiḥâd al-Madâris al-Islâmîyah al-Ahlîyah (Association of Islamic Private Schools), has been recognized and accredited by the Arab Muslim countries. This means that a student with a high secondary Arabic-religious certificate can continue education in the first year of the Middle Eastern university program because the system fits his background without any difficulty or mismatching.

To comply with the national policy of educational reform, the religious teachers have to adjust their institution's systems skillfully. Without proper adjustment, the pondok or the madrasah might be left out of the revised national educational system which requires a basic education in Thai and general subjects (referred to earlier as 'Thai education'). To accept the Thai education components without good preparation, as proposed by the government seems to be a double-edged sword. This is because Thai education programs in Islamic private schools in the early period lacked qualified personnel when compared to public schools. The required subjects, when offered in the Islamic private schools, are normally lower in standard than those of public schools. The religious teachers realize that the introduction of Thai education by the government into the Muslim institution is, besides upgrading the education for Muslims in southern Thailand, intended to make them feel more 'Thai' than 'Malay'. The government also hopes that Thai education may cause Thai to supersede the Malay language.

However, the actual outcome of the government's efforts shows that the students of the Islamic private schools of southern Thailand have now mastered both Thai and Malay, in addition to the Arabic that is offered as the main subject in those schools. In fact, the Malay language taught in these schools follows closely the standards of the same subject in Malaysia and Indonesia. The reason behind this is that most of the Arabic teachers (ustaz) speak Malay as a means of making the Arabic subjects understandable to their students. These teachers are initially trained by Malay instructors, though most of them are the graduates of Middle Eastern universities. The teachers who are the alumni of Indonesian universities play an effective role in refining the students' accents towards those of the Indonesian dialect, which is regarded as a more standard dialect. So, with the open-eyed adaptation of the pondok and madarasah into the national educational reform program of the government, the students of the Islamic private schools can develop their language skills in both Thai and Malay to a satisfactory and acceptable level.

In order to make the mention policy of educational reform more effective, the government established an educational center in Yala, south Thailand, for launching the policy. The area this center has within its authority is known as Educational Region Two. The main aim of this center is to introduce and supervise Thai education in the Islamic private schools. It also functions as a guardian of all aspects of the educational process involving the Thai and Arabic-religious educations. Moreover, the center expects to bring more Muslim children into public schools, as well as to have their parents' approval, knowing well that the Muslim parents would prefer to send their children to the pondok or the more religious institution. In order to win their approbation, the center provides an Islamic studies program in public schools ranging from the first to the six elementary levels. The program satisfies the parents because their children learn to understand the basic principles of Islam while they are following the Thai education system. The Islamic studies program in the public schools seems to bring the Muslim children more to an Islamic orientation than to a Thai cultural one in many ways. What is right and what is wrong, as it is seen from the perspective of Islam, becomes clear to them and they try to avoid practicing what seems to be un-Islamic. The resulting attitude, as such, creates an unsatisfactory condition in the view of the Thai authorities. The fact is that instead of adopting Thai culture as expected, the Muslim children of the southern border provinces of Thailand keep practicing Islam and the Islamic culture in its Malay variety. A small example can be seen when the children keep on using *assalamu'alaikum* as an Islamic greeting to their parents and relatives instead of raising their hands up to their chest, pressing the flat of their palms together, with a little bow of the head as a sign of respect as is done in the Thai culture.

This phenomenon creates a new atmosphere in the public schools that has never existed before. The phenomenon, as such, is in fact, a continuation of what has been taught in the Muslim community of southern Thailand. The personnel of the Educational Region Two Administration suggest that the Islamic studies program be extended into every public school in which Muslims students form over fifty percent of the intake. They also recommend that the government keep on providing such programs, continuing through the secondary, vocational, college and the university levels. However, the government seem to be reluctant to provide such a program on a wider basis than that currently implemented in the southern provinces.

As to the Arabic-religious education provided in the Islamic private schools in the four southern border provinces of Thailand, we find that the religious teachers have fixed their long term aims on upgrading their institutions to a higher level. They anticipate that the secondary level (*thânawîyah*) would likely have added to it another step in educational system known as *al-'âlî*, which equals a two-year diploma degree. The fact is that some of the Islamic private schools in the four southern border provinces of Thailand have already launched such a program. Furthermore, the Muslims of southern Thailand need to have a special higher institution of a modern type that can accommodate the enrollments of graduates from the Islamic private schools. The institution is aiming to have courses in some of the traditional Islamic disciplines included in all programs of learning as a basic requirement.

In fact, there is a movement among the Muslim scholars in southern Thailand to set up a private college level where the Islamic world view provided a foundation for the higher education of the Muslim students in many vocational, academic, and professional fields. It would be interesting to speculate upon the response and reaction of the Thai government on the issue at this time. How will the government deal with this? Will the movement be curbed or ignored? Or will the government be willing to meet the Muslim scholars halfway? Whatever the response, the outcome will certainly be significant in the history of the Muslim approach towards educational development in Thailand.

Plate 1. The arch of Pondok Berming

Plate 2. Pondok Berming

Plate 3. The sign board to the Islamic charity body in Pondok Dalo

Plate 4. This is called Pondok Dalae in the vicinity of Pondok Dalo. Pondok
Dalae are meant for married couples only

Plate 5. Pondok Babayeh in Toyong, Patani

Plate 6. The entrance to Pondok Mak Dagae

Plate 7. Pondok Haji Mak Dagae in Naprado, Patani

Plate 8. The house of Tuan Guru Haji Mak Dagae

Plate 9. The *Balaisah* in Pondok Mango

Plate 10. This is the sign of *Makam Syuhada* Dato' Panglima Kampong
Tok Semla Patani Darulsalam in Pondok Semla

Plate 11. The Islamic Committee of Patani

Plate 12. Darulma'arif Institute, in the Patronage by the Islamic
Committee of Patani

Plate 13. Arabic School known as Darun Sat School in Saiburu, Patani

Plate 14. College of Islamic Studies, Prince of Songkla University, Patani

Plate 15. Saudara Press, serve as both the bookstore and printing house

Plate 16. Taman Pustaka Press, produces the works of the present generation
of religious teachers of Patani

Plate 17. Haris Trading was opened in 1939, distributing
religious books to the pondok in various parts of Patani

Plate 18. Mohammad Nahdi Bookstore, one of the Muslim bookstore in
downtown area of Patani

Plate 19. Masjid Jamek Patani

Plate 20. Masjid Cabang Tiga Patani

منهاج العابدين

الى جنة رب العالمين

فدبجارا الصوف يغ مترجمه دغن بهاس ملايو اوله العالم العلامة العارف

الرباني مولانا وقدوتنا الشيخ داود بن عبدالله الفطاني

يأت ترجمه درفد كتاب منهاج العابدين بك

حجة الاسلام الغزالي الطوسي تغمدهما

الله تعالى برحمته

آمين

{ حقوق الطبع محفوظة }

مكتبة ومطبعة محمد النهدي واولاده
٧-٦٧٩/٩ شارع اسرابب سيكينك بانكوك – تايلاند
تليفون : ١٦٦١٨٤١٧

Plate 21. Kitab *Minhaj al-Abidin ila Jannat Rabb al-Amin*

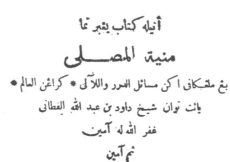

أينله كتاب يڤربر نما

منية المصلى

بۏ ملتكاڤى ا كن مسائل السرر واللآلى ٭ كراغن العالم ٭

يائت توان شيخ داود بن عبد الله الفطانى

غفر الله له آمين

ثم آمين

دان أواله فد آخر كتاب اين ساتو رسالة يۏد نما كندى البهجة المرضية

فد بجارا موافق دان تخالف مأموم ا كن امام ترجمة الشيخ داود بن

عبد الله الفطانى المذكور غفر الله له ولوالديه ولجميع المسلمين آمين

مكتبة ومطبعة محمد النهدى واولاده

٦٧٩/٦-٧ ڤارع اسوراب سيكينتكيك باتكوك ــ تايلانده

تليفون : ٤٦٦٤٨٤٧

Plate 22. Kitab *Munyat al-Musalli* by Shaykh Dawud
bin Abdullah al-Fatani

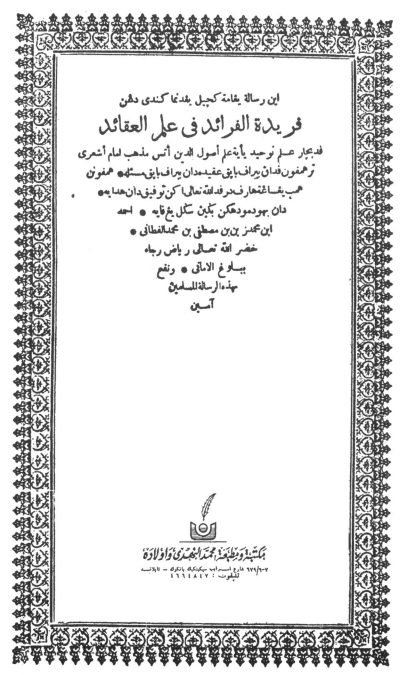

Plate 23. Kitab *Faridat al-Faraid fi Ilm al-Aqaaid by Shaykh Ahmad bin Muhammad Zayn bin Mustafa al-Fatani*

ابن سوات كتاب يغمبيل بهامث فندبق عبارتين لاكي أمت بناكل كهندفن
لاكي ايلق اتوراين دنماكندي

بهجة المبتدين وفرحة المجتدين

فد بجارا علم أمول الدين دان علمنقه درفد بغ بركتنوغ دئن
عبادة دان معاملات دان لاين درفد كدوان دان دهولو درفد
دمكين ايت سوات، مقدمه فدكلبيهن علم دان اهلين
درفد بيراف حديث دان لاين دان فداخر كتاب
اين دواخاتمه، ملك خاتمه يغ فرتماقدمبتاكن
بيراف فرائعي يغ ايلق دان خاتمه يغكدوا
فد سوات فوتوغ درفد علم تصوف
همغون ئن الفقير الى عفوالله تعالى
احمد بن محمد زين ابن
مصطفى بن محمد
الفطاني
عفى الله تعالى عنهم وعن املا قهم ومحييهم اجمعين امين

دان فدتفين بيراف حاشيه اتس اين كتاب تله ملغكافي اي اتس بيراف
مسائل يغ ايلق دسورتكندي اوله موءلفن عفى الله تعالى عنه امين

كتاب اين تله درجشرركن ملك تياد دبنتركن باڬي سياف ٢ هچف كتاب
اين ملينكن دئن اذن دان رضا درفد ا نق فغارغ ن يأيت حاج وان اسماعيل
بن احمد فطاني دان بارغسياف مغجف تيدق دئن كبنران اكن دعوى
اتس ن دان تيف ٢ نسخه يغ تياد فدان جف وارئن دبيلغكندي ترجوري

مكتبة ومطبعة محمد النهدي واولاده
٧-٦٧٩/٦ تاريخ اسراب بيكتبكه بانكوك — تايلاند
تلفون: ٤٦٦١٨٤٧

Plate 25. Kitab *Kashf al-Litham an Asilat al-Anam*

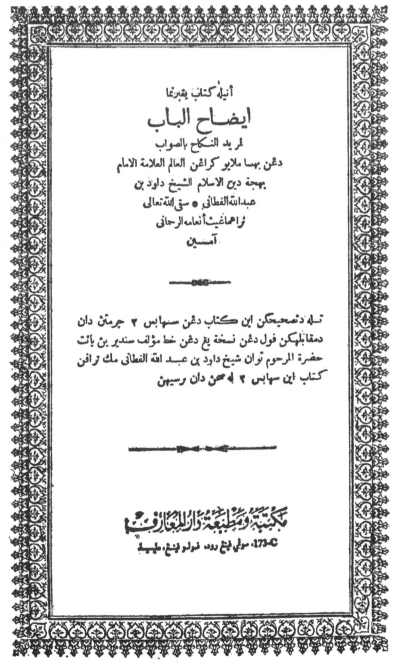

أنيله كتاب يڬرنما

ايضاح الباب

لمريد النكاح بالصواب

دغن بهسا ملايو كراڠن العالم العلامة الامام
بهجة دين الاسلام الشيخ داود بن
عبدالله الفطاني ۞ سقى الله تعالى
ثراهما غيث أنعامه الرحاني
آمين

تـله دتصحيحكن اين كتاب دغن سهابس ۲ جرمتن دان
دمقابلهكن فول دغن نسخة يڬ دغن خط مؤلف سنديرى ين بائت
حضـرة المرحوم توان شيخ داود بن عبـد الله الفطاني ملك تراڤن
كتاب اين سهابس ۲ له محن دان رسيمن

مكتبة ومطبعة دار المعارف
C-173، سوقى فنج دودو ڤولو ڤنڠ، مليبيه

Plate 26. Kitab *Idah al-Bab li-Murid al-Nikah bi-al-Sawab*

Bibliography

Abbas, Ihsan. 1980. Some Aspects of Social Life in Andalusia during the Time of the Almoravides in the Light of the *Nawâzil* of Ibn Rushd. *Zeitschrift der deutschen morgenandischen Gesellschaft*. Supplement 5, 24(29): 155-65.

Ackerman, S. E. and R. L.M. Lee. 1988. *Heaven in Transition: Non-Muslim Religious Innovation and Ethnic Identity in Malaysia*. Honolulu: University of Hawaii Press.

Adams, C. C. 1968. *Islam and Modernism in Egypt: A Study of the Modern Movement Inaugurated by Muḥammad 'Abduh*. New York: Russell & Russell.

Adams, D. K. 1966. *Introduction to Education: A Comparative Analysis*. California: Wadsworth Publishing Company, Inc.

Alatas, Syed Faris. 1985. Notes on Various Theories Regarding the Islamization of the Malay Archipelago. *The Muslim World*. 75: 162-75.

Al-Attas, Syed Naquib. 1969. *Preliminary Statement on a General Theory of the Islamization of the Malay-Indonesia Archipelago*. Kuala Lumpur: Dewan Bahasa dan Pustaka.

'Alî, 'Abdullah Yûsuf. 1989. *The Holy Qur'ân*. Maryland: Amana Corporation.

Alpern, S. I. 1974. The Thai Muslims. *Asian Affairs*. 1: 246-54.

Annandale, N. 1904. The People of the Malay Peninsula. *The Scottish Geographical Magazine*. 20: 334-48.

Battle, J.A. and R.L. Shannon. 1974. *The New Idea in Education*. London: Harper & Row Publishers.

Beg, Muhammad Abdul Jabbar. 1983. *Arabic Loan-Words in Malay: A Survey of Arabic and Islamic Influence Upon the Languages of Mankind*. Kuala Lumpur: The University of Malaya Press.

Blagden, C.O. 1917. Summaries of Lectures Delivered at the School. *Bulletin of the School of Oriental Studies*. 1: 97-100.

Blanchard, W. 1958. *Thailand: Its People, Its Society, Its Culture*. New Haven: HRAF Press.

Bolan, B.J. 1971. *The Struggle of Islam in Modern Indonesia*. The Hague: Martinus Nijhoff.

Bock, J. C. 1982. Education and Development: A Conflict of Meaning. In *Comparative Education*, edited by Philip G. Altbach, Robert F. Arnove, Gail P. Kelly. New York: MacMillan Publishing Co.

Bougas, W. 1986. Some Early Islamic Tombstones in Pattani. *Journal of the Malaysian Branch of the Royal Asiatic Society*. 59(1): 85-112.

Buchanan, K. 1967. *The Southeast Asian World*. New York: Taplinger Publishing Company.

Burr, A. 1977. Group Ideology, Consciousness and Social Problems: A Study of Buddhist and Muslim Concepts of Sin in Two Southern Thai Coastal Fishing Villages. *Anthropos*. 62 (3-4): 433-46.

Burr, A. 1977. Religious Institutional Diversity-Social Structural and Conceptual Unity: Islam and Buddhism in a Southern Thai Coastal Fishing Village. *Journal of the Siam Society*. 60(2): 183-215.

Chandran, J. 1965. British Foreign Policy and the Extraterritorial Question in Siam 1891-1900. *Royal Asiatic Society of Great Britain & Ireland, Malayan Branch Singapore Journal.* 32(2): 290-313.

Chee Meow, Seah. 1974. The Muslim Issue and Implications. *Pacific Community.* (1): 139-60.

Cook, D. R. and N. K. LaFleur. 1975. *A Guide to Educational Research.* 2nd. ed. Boston: Allyn and Bacon. Inc.

Cooper, R.L. 1982. *Language Spread: Studies in Diffusion and Social Change.* Washington: Indiana University Press.

Cortes, R.M. 1984. A Preliminary Study of Modernizing Trends in Muslim Education in Indonesia and the Philippines: A Special Focus on the Pesantren Tradition in Java. *Southeast Asian Studies Program Report* 1: 1-75.

Dhofier, Z. 1980. The Pesantren Tradition: A Study of the Role of the Kyai in the Maintenance of the Traditional Ideology of Islam in Java. Ph.D. dissertation, Canberra, The Australian National University.

Dhofier, Z. 1980. Kinship and Marriage among the Javanese Kyai. *Indonesia.* 29 (April): 47-58.

Dodge, B. 1962. *Muslim Education in Medieval Times.* Washington: Middle East Institute.

Donner, W. 1987. *The Five Faces of Thailand.* New York: St. Martin's Press.

Dulyakasem, U. 1981. Education and Ethnic Nationalism: *A Study of the Muslim-Malays in Southern Siam.* Ann Arbor: Michigan University.

Dulyakasem, U. 1984. Muslim-Malay Separatism in Southern Thailand: Factors underlying the political Revolt. In *Armed Separatism in Southeast Asia,* edited by Lim Joo Jock and Vanis. Singapore: Institute of Southeast Asian Studies.

Engeneer, Asghar Ali. 1983. Islam in Thailand-Resurgence or Consolidation. *Islam and the Modern Age.* 14(1) (February): 59-67.

Esposito, J. L. (ed). 1983. *Voices of Resurgent Islam.* Oxford: Oxford University Press.

Esposito, J. L. 1981. The Muslim of Thailand. *Islamika.* Kuala Lumpur: Percetakan United Selangor.

Fatimi, S.Q. 1963. *Islam Comes to Malaysia.* Singapore: Malaysian Sociological Research Institute Ltd.

Federspiel, H. M. 1985. Islam and Development in the Nations of Asean. *Asian Survey.* 25(8): 805-21.

Federspiel, H. M. 1970. The Muhammadijah: A Study of an Orthodox Islamic Movement in Indonesia. *Indonesia.* 10 (October): 57-80.

Fischer, M. 1982. Islam and the Revolt of the Petit Bourgeoisie. *Daedalus: Journal of the American Academy of Arts and Sciences.* 111(1): 101-25.

Floris, P. 1934. *Voyage to the East Indies in the Globe 1611-1615.* London: The Hakluyt Society.

Forbes, A. D.W. 1982. Thailand's Muslim Minorities: Assimilation, Succession, Or Coexistence? *Asian Survey.* 22(11) November: 1056-73.

Fraser, T. M. Jr. 1960. *Rusembilan: A Malay Fishing Village in Southern Thailand.* Ithaca: Cornell University Press.

Fraser, T. M. Jr. 1966. *Fishermen of South Thailand: The Malay-Villagers.* New York: Holt, Rinehart and Winston, Inc.

Galzer, N. & Daniel P. M., eds. 1976. *Ethnicity: Theory and Experience.* Cambridge: Harvard University Press.

Golomb, L. 1985. Curing and Sociocultural Separatism in South Thailand. *Social Science and Medicine.* 21(4): 463-68.

Gowing, P. G. 1982. Muslims in the Philippines, Religion and Regional Cooperation: The Mindanao Problem and Asean. *Journal of the Institute of Muslim Minority Affairs.* 4(1, 2): 14-23.

Haddad, Wadi D. 1980. *Education: Sector Policy Paper.* 3rd edition. Washington D.C.: World Bank.

Haemindra, Nantawan. 1976. The Problem of the Thai-Muslims in the Four Southern Provinces of Thailand, Part 1. *Journal of Southeast Asian Studies.* 7(2) 197-225.

Haemindra, Nantawan. 1977. The Problem of the Thai Muslims in the Four Southern Provinces of Thailand, Part 2, *Journal of Southeast Asian Studies.* 8(1): 85-105.

Hall, D.G.E. 1955. *A History of South-East Asia.* New York: MacMillan.

Hamid al-Afendi, Muhammad & Nabi Ahmad Balcon, eds. 1980. *Curriculum and Teacher Education.* Jeddah: King Abdulaziz University.

Harrison, B. 1954. *South-East Asia: A Short History.* London: MacMillan.

Hurgronje, C. S. 1931. *Mekka in the Latter Part of the 19th Century.* Translated by J.H. Monahan. London: Luzac & Co.

Ibn Khaldun. 1958. *The Muqaddimah: An Introduction to History.* Translated by Franz Rosenthal. New York: Pantheon Books Inc.

Ibrahim, Ahmad., Sharon Siddique, & Yasmin Hussain, eds. 1986. *Readings on Islam in Southeast Asia.* Singapore: Institute of Southeast Asian Studies.

Israeli, R., ed. 1982. *The Cresent in the East: Islam in Asia Minor.* London: Curzon Press Ltd.

Jeshurun, C. 1972. Lord Landsdowne and the 'Anti-German Clique' at the Foreign Office: Their Role in the making of the Anglo-Siamese Agreement of 1902. *Journal of Southeast Asian Studies.* 3(2): 229-46.

Jha, G. 1978. Muslim Minorities in the Philippines and Thailand. *India Quarterly.* 34(3): 328-46.

Johns, A.H. 1981. From Coastal Settlement to Islamic School and City: Islamization in Sumatra, The Malay Peninsula and Java. *Hamdard Islamicus.* 2(4): 3-24.

Johns, A.H. 1984. Islam in the Malay World: An Exploratory Survey with Some Reference to Qur'anic Exegesis. *Islam in Asia,* edited by Raphael Israeli and Anthony H. Johns. Boulder: Westview.

Johns, A.H. 1976. Islam in Southeast Asia: Problems of Perspective, *Southeast Asian History and Historiography,* edited by C.D. Cowan & O.W. Wolters. Ithaca: Cornell University Press.

Jones, R. 1979. Ten Conversion Myths from Indonesia. *Conversion to Islam,* edited by Nehemia Levtzion. New York, London: Holmes & Meier Publishers, Inc.

Kettani, M. Ali. 1986. *Muslim Minorities in the World Today.* London: Mansell Publications Ltd.

Keyes, C. F. 1987. *Thailand: Buddhist Kingdom as Modern Nation-State.* Boulder: Westview Press.

Kiernan, Y.G. 1955. Britain, Siam, and Malaya: 1875-1885. *The Journal of Modern History* 28(1) (March): 1-20.

Koch, M. L. 1977. Patani and the Development of a Thai State. *Journal of the Malayan Branch of the Royal Asiatic Society.* 50(2): 69-88.

Landau, R. 1958. *Islam and the Arabs.* London: George Allen & Unwin Ltd.

Landon, K. Perry. 1968. *Siam in Transition.* New York: Greenwood Press, Publisher.

Leng, Lee Yong. 1980. Race, Language, and National Cohesion in Southeast Asia. *Journal of Southeast Asian Studies.* 11(1): 112-38.

Levtzion, N., ed. 1979. *Conversion to Islam.* New York: Holmes & Meier Publishers.

Lewis, B., V.L. Menage, Ch. Pellat & J. Schacht, eds. 1971. *The Islamic Encyclopaedia of Islam.* New Edition. Leiden: E.J. Brill and Luzac & Co.

Lewis, B, Ch. Pellat & J. Schacht, eds. 1965 *The Encyclopedia of Islam.* London: E.J. Brill and Luzac & co.

Makdisi, G. 1981. *The Rise of Colleges: Institutions of Learning in Islam and the West.* Edinburgh: Edinburgh University Press.

Matheson, V. and M.B. Hooker. Jawi Literature in Patani: The Maintenance of an Islamic Tradition. 1988. *Journal of the Malaysian Branch of the Royal Asiatic Society.* 61 (254): 1-86.

Mathur, Y.B. 1968. Muslim in Siam 1900-1925. *Studies in Islam* (October): 220-231.

Means, G. P. 1978. Public Policy toward Religion in Malaysia. *Pacific Affairs.* 51(3): 348-405.

Means, G. P., ed. 1977. *Development and Underdevelopment in Southeast Asia.* Ottawa: Canadian Council for Southeast Asian Studies.

Mills, J.V. 1930. Eredia's description of Malaca. *Journal of the Malayan Branch of the Royal Asiatic Society* 8(1): 17-58.

Mills, L. and associates. 1949. *The New World of Southeast Asia.* Minneapolis: The University of Minnesota Press.

Mohd. Nor bin Ngah. 1982. *Kitab Jawi: Islamic Thought of the Malay Muslim Scholars,* No. 33. Singapore: Institute of Southeast Asian Studies.

Mudmarn, Saynee. 1988. Language Use and Language Loyalty among the Muslim-Malays of Southern Thailand. Ph.D. dissertation, The State University of New York at Buffalo.

Muhammad Kamal Hassan. 1982. *Muslim Intellectual Responses to 'New Order' Modernization in Indonesia.* Kuala Lumpur: Dewan Bahasa dan Pustaka.

Nagata, J. 1980. Religious Ideology and Social Change: The Islamic revival in Malaysia. *Pacific Affairs.* 53(3): 405-39.

Nation (Bangkok). 31 October 1974.

Nation (Bangkok). 15 December 1980.

Newbold, T.J. 1971. *British Settlements in the Straits of Malacca,* Vol. 2. London: Oxford University Press.

Nieuwenhuijze, C.A.O. Van. 1957. *Aspects of Islam in Post-Colonial Indonesia.* The Hague: W. Van Hoeve Ltd.

Noss, R. B., ed. 1984. *An Overview of Language Issues in Southeast Asia 1950-1980.* Oxford: Oxford University Press.

Ochsenwald, W. 1984. *Religion, Society and the State in Arabia: The Hijaz under Ottoman Control, 1840-1908.* Columbus: Ohio State University Press.

Omar Farouk. 1984. The Historical and Traditional Dimensions of Malay-Muslim Separatism in Southern Thailand. In *Armed Separatism in Southeast Asia,* edited by Lim Joo Jock and Vanis. Singapore: Institute of Southeast Asian Studies.

Orr, Kenneth, M.M. Billah & Budi Lazarusli. 1977. Education for This Life or for the Life to Come: Observations on the Javanese Village Madrasah. *Indonesia.* 14 (April): 129-56.

Pitsuwan, Surin. 1982. Islam and Malay Nationalism: A Case Study of the Malay-Muslims of Southern Thailand. Ph.D. dissertation, Harvard University, Cambridge.

Prachobmoh, Chavivun. 1982. Ethnic relations among Thai, Thai Muslim and Chinese in South Thailand. In *Ethnicity and Interpersonal Interaction,* edited by David Y. H. Wu. Singapore: Maruzen Asia.

Rahman, Fazlur. 1978. *Islam.* Chicago: University of Chicago Press.

Rippin, A., ed. 1988. *Approaches to the History of the Interpretation of the Qur'an.* Oxford: Clarendon Press.

Robequain, C. 1958. *Malaya, Indonesia, Borneo and the Philippines.* Translated by E.D. Laborde. London: Longmans.

Roff, W. R., ed. 1974. *Kelantan: Religion, Society and Politics in a Malay State.* Kuala Lumpur: Oxford University Press.

_____. 1970. Indonesian and Malay Students in Cairo in the 1920's. *Indonesia.* 9 (April): 73-88.

Satha-Anand, Chaiwat. 1983. *Islam and Violence: A Case Study of Violent Events in the Four Southern Provinces, Thailand 1976-1981.* Bangkok: Thai Khadi Research Institute.

Scupin, R. 1980. The Politics of Islamic Reformism in Thailand. *Asian Survey.* 20 (December): 1223-35.

Scupin, R. 1982. The Social Significance of the *Hajj* for Thai Muslims. *The Muslim World.* 72(1) January: 25-33.

Scupin, R. 1981. The Socio-Economic Status of Muslims in Central and North Thailand. *Journal of Institute of Muslim Minority Affairs.* 3(2) Winter: 163-189.

Seyyed Hossein Nasr. 1987. *Traditional Islam in the Modern World.* London: KPI.

Soedjatmoko. 1850. A Case Study in Cultural Contents: The Malay Language. *South Asia in the World Today,* edited by Philips Talbot. Chicago: The University of Chicago Press.

Shushtery, A.M.A. 1938. *Outlines of Islamic Culture: Historical and Cultural Aspects.* Vol. 1. Bangalore City: The Bangalore Press.

Suhrke, A. & Lela G. N. 1977. Muslims in the Philippines and Thailand. In *Ethnic Conflict in International Relations,* edited by Suhrke A. and Lela, G. N. New York: Praeger Publishers.

Suhrke, A. 1977. Loyalists and Separatists: The Muslims in Southern Thailand. *Asian Survey.* 17(3) March: 237-306.

Suhrke, A. 1981. Thailand. *The Politics of Islamic Reassertion,* edited by Mohammad Ayoob. New York: St. Martin's Press.

Suhrke, A. 1973. The Thai-Muslim Border Provinces: Some National Security Aspects. *Studies of Contemporary Thailand,* edited by Robert Ho, and E.C. Chapman. Canberra: Australian University Press.

Suseendirarajah, S. 1980. Religion and Language in Jaffna Society. *Anthropological Linguistics.* 22(8) November: 345-362.

Syukri, Ibrahim. 1985. *History of the Malay Kingdom of Patani.* Translated by Corner Bailey & John N. Miksic. Ohio University: Ohio University Press.

Taylor, R. 1961. *The Empiricists.* New York: Doubleday & Company.

Thailand: Official Year Book 1964. 1964. Bangkok: Government House Printing Office.

Thimkhan, Pawee (Thawee), Dolmanach Baka, and Phayom Petkla. 1987. *Muslim*

Society, Higher Education and Development: The Case Study of Thailand. Singapore: Institute of Southeast Asian Studies.

Ladd, T. M. 1974. Bureaucratic Attitudes and Behavior as Obstacles to Political Intergration of Thai Muslims. *Southeast Asia.* 3(1): 545-66.

Ladd, T. M. 1977. The Malayan Communist Insurgent and Thai-Malaysian Relations. *Asian Affairs* (July-August): 306-16.

Ladd, T. M. 1977. The Malayan Communist Insurgency. *Asian Affairs* (May-June): 306-16.

Ladd, T. M. 1969. *Socio-Economic Approach to Political Integration of the Thai-Islam: An Appraisal.* N00014-66-C0176. Northern Illinois University and Center for Southeast Asian Studies.

Ladd, T. M. 1966. Political Socialization of the Thai-Islam. *Studies on Asia,* 7: 89-105.

Ladd, T. M. 1975. *Political Violence in the Muslim Provinces of Southern Thailand.* Singapore: Institute of Southeast Asian Studies.

Thompson, V. 1941. *Thailand: The new Siam.* New York: The MacMillan Company.

Teeuw, A., & D.K. Wyatt. 1970. *The Story of Patani.* The Haque: Matinus Nijhoff.

Walker, D. Conflict between the Thai and Islamic Cultures in Southern Thailand 1948-1970. *Studies in Islam.* 9(3-4): 135-153.

Wan Kadir bin Che Man. 1983. The Muslim Elites and Politics in Southern Thailand. M.A. thesis, Universiti Sains Malaysia.

Weekes, R. V., ed. 1984. *Muslim People: A World Ethnographic Survey.* (Second edition) Connecticut: Greenwood Press.

Wilson, H.E. 1985. Partisan Imperialist and Islamic Separatism in South Thailand, 1945-49. *Canadian Journal of History.*20: 369-391.

Winstedt, R. S. 1969. *A History of Classical Malay Literature.* Kuala Lumpur, Oxford University Press.

Winzeler, R. L. 1985. *Ethnic Relations in Kelantan: A Study of the Chinese and Thai as Ethnic Minorities in a Malay State.* Singapore, Oxford University Press.

Winzeler, R. L. 1975. Traditional Islamic Schools in Kelantan. *Journal of the Malaysian Branch of the Royal Asiatic Society.* 48(1): 91-103.

Malay Sources and Kitâb Jâwî

Abdul Rahman al-Ahmadi. 1984. Sejarah Hubungan Kelantan/Patani dengan Sulawesi Selatan. *Warisan Kelantan* oleh Nik Mohamad bin Nik Mohammad Salleh. Kota Bharu, Kelantan: Perbadanan Muzium Negeri Kelantan.

Badriyah Haji Salleh. 1984. *Kampong Haji Salleh dan Madrasah Saadiah-Salihiah* 1914-1959. Kuala Lumpur: Dewan Bahasa dan Pustaka Bahasa.

Khoo K.K. 1982. *Beberapa Aspek Warisan Kelantan* I. Kota Bharu: Perbadanan Muzium Negeri Kelantan.

Khoo K.K. 1983. *Beberapa Aspek Warisan Kelantan* II. Kota Bharu: Perbadanan Muzium Negeri Kelantan.

Kyai Shaykh Muhammad Arshad al-Banjârî. n.d. *Sabîl al-Muhtadîn lil-Tafaqquh fî-Amr al-Dîn.* Penang: Maktabat wa-Matba'at Dâr al-Ma'ârif, n.d.

Mana Sikana. 1983. *Sastera Islam di Malaysia.* Kuala Lumpur: Art Printing Works Sdn. Bhd.

Muhammad Nûr bin Ismâ'îl al-Fatânî. n.d. *Kifâyat al-Muhtadî,* Penang: Maktabat wa-Matba'at Dâr al-Ma'ârif.

Nia'mat Yusuff. 1984. "Kepentingan Tarbiyah Islamiyah Dalam Pembentukan Manusia yang Sempurna." Paper presented at Seminar Pendidikan Islam (Pondok), Anjuran Persatuan Mahasiswa Islam UPM., dengan kerjasama Unit Bimbingan Agama, HEP, UPM, Malaysia, 6-7 October.

Nik Abdul Aziz bin Haji Nik Hassan. 1983. *Islam di Kelantan.* Kuala Lumpur: United Selangor Press.

Nik Abdul Aziz bin Haji Nik Hassan. 1977. *Sejarah Perkembangan 'Ulamâ' Kelantan.* Kota Bharu: Pustaka Aman Press Sdn. Bhd.

Rahardjo, M. Dawam, ed. 1974. *Pesantren dan Pembaharuan.* Jakarta: Penarbit LP3ES.

Sabri Haji Said. 1983. *Madrasah al-Ulum al-Syarî'ah Perak: Satu kajian pendidikan Islam.* Kuala Lumpur: Dewan Bahasa dan Pustaka.

Sa'ad Shuri bin Haji Muda. 1971. *Detik-detik Sejarah Kelantan.* Kota Bharu: Pustaka Aman Press.

Shafie bin Abu Bakar. 1984. Konsep Ilmu di dalam Islam: Peranan dan Sumbangan Institusi Pendidikan Islam Pondok Tradisional dalam Sejarah Pendidikan Umat Islam di Malaysia. Paper presented at Seminar Pendidikan Islam (Pondok), anjuran Persatuan Mahasiswa Islam UPM., dengan kerjasama Unit Bimbingan Agama, HEP, UPM, Malaysia, 6-7 October.

Shaykh Aḥmad bin Muḥammad Zayn bin Muṣtafá al-Faṭânî. n.d. *Farîdat al-Farâ'id fî-'Ilm al-'Aqâ'id.* Penang: Maktabat wa-Maṭba'at Dâr al-Ma'ârif, n.d.

Shaykh Aḥmad bin Muḥammad Zayn bin Muṣtafá al-Faṭânî. n.d. *Bahjat al-Mubtadîn wa-Farḥat al-Mujtadîn.* Penang: Maktabat wa-Maṭba'at Dâr al-Ma'ârif.

Shaykh Aḥmad bin Muḥammad Zayn bin Muṣtafá al-Faṭânî. n.d. *Abniyat al-Asmâ' wa-al-Af'âl.* Penang: Maktabat wa-Matba'at Dâr al-Ma'ârif.

Shaykh Aḥmad bin Muḥammad Zayn bin Muṣtafá al-Faṭânî. n.d. 1958. *al-Fatâwâ al-Faṭânîyah.* Pattani: Pattani Press.

Shaykh Aḥmad bin Muḥammad Zayn bin Muṣtafá al-Faṭânî. n.d. 1954. *Ṭîb al-Iḥsân fî-Ṭibb al-Insân.* Penang: Persama Press.

Shaykh Aḥmad bin Muḥammad Zayn bin Muṣtafá al-Faṭânî. n.d. *Luqṭat al-'Ajalân Fîmâ Tamassu Ilayhî Ḥâjat al-Insân.* Penang: Persama Press, n.d.

Shaykh Dâwûd bin 'Abd Allâh bin Idrîs al-Faṭânî. n.d. *Furû' al-Masâ'il.* Penang: Maktabat wa-Maṭba'at Dâr al-Ma'ârif.

Shaykh Dâwûd bin 'Abd Allâh bin Idrîs al-Faṭânî. n.d. *Bughyat al-Ṭullâb li-Murîd al-Ma'rifat al-Aḥkâm bi-al-Ṣawâb.* Penang: Maktabat wa-Maṭba'at Dâr al-Ma'ârif.

Shaykh Dâwûd bin 'Abd Allâh bin Idrîs al-Faṭânî. n.d. *Minhâj al-'Âbidîn ilâ Jannat Rabb al-'Alamîn.* Penang: Maktabat wa-Maṭba'ât Dâr al-Ma'ârif.

Shaykh Dâwûd bin 'Abd Allâh bin Idrîs al-Faṭânî. n.d. *al-Durr al-Thamîn.* Penang: Maktabat wa-Maṭba'at Dâr al-Ma'ârif.

Shaykh Dâwûd bin 'Abd Allâh bin Idrîs al-Faṭânî. n.d. *Munyat al-Musallî.* Penang: Maktabat wa-Maṭba'at Dâr al-Ma'ârif.

Shaykh Dâwûd bin 'Abd Allâh bin Idrîs al-Faṭânî. n.d. *Sullam al-Mubtadî.* Penang: Maktabat wa-Maṭba'at Dâr al-Ma'ârif.

Shaykh Dâwûd bin 'Abd Allâh bin Idrîs al-Faṭânî. n.d. *Idâh al-Bâb.* Penang: Maktabat wa-Maṭba'at Dâr al-Ma'ârif.

Shaykh Dâwûd bin 'Abd Allâh bin Idrîs al-Faṭânî. n.d. *Kifâyat al-Muḥtâj.* Penang: Maktabat wa-Maṭba'at Dâr al-Ma'ârif.

Shaykh Muḥammad bin Ismâ'il Dâwûd al-Faṭânî, n.d. *Maṭla' al-Badrayn wa-Majma' al al-Baḥrayn.* Penang: Maktabat wa-Maṭba'at Dâr al-Ma'ârif, n.d.

Shaykh Muhammad bin Ismâ'il Dâwûd al-Fatânî, n.d. *Wishâh al-Afrâh wa-Isbâh al-Falâh*. Penang: Maktabat wa-Matba'at Dâr al-Ma'ârif.

Shaykh Zayn al-'Abidîn bin Muhammad al-Fatânî. n.d. *Kashf al-Lithâm 'an As'ilat al-Anâm*. Singapore: Sulayman Mar'î.

Shaykh Zayn al-'Abidîn bin Muhammad al-Fatânî. n.d. *'Aqîdat al-Nâjîn*. Penang: Maktabat wa-Matba'at Dâr al-Ma'ârif.

Shaykh Zayn al-'Abidîn bin Muhammad al-Fatânî. n.d. *Kashf al-Ghâybîyah*. Penang: Maktabat wa-Matba'at Dâr al-Ma'ârif, n.d.

Shaykh Zayn al-'Abidîn bin Muhammad al-Fatânî. n.d. *Irshâd al-'Ibâd ilâ Sabîl al-Rashâd*. Penang: Maktabat wa-Matba'at Dâr al-Ma'ârif.

Uthmân bin 'Abd Allah. n.d. *Kitab Sifat Dua Puluh*. (Book of Twenty Attributes). Penang; Maktabat wa Matba'at Dâr al-Ma'ârif.

Wan Muhammad Saghîr 'Abd Allâh (Ustâdh). 1979. *Sufi dan Waliyullah*. (Sufi and Waliyullah). Kota Bharu, Kelantan: Pustaka Aman Press.

Thai Sources

Abdulkadir, Mohammad. 1977. *An Introduction to Islam and Muslim in Four Southern Provinces* '(Bangkoknoi)': Aksornpandit.

Anantakul, Anant. 1983. *Nayobai kiaw kab kuam mankong nai changwat chaiden pak tai*. (Policy of the security problem in the southern border provinces). Paper presented at Kosit Hotel, Hat Yai, Songkhla, South Thailand.

Bangnara, A. 1976. *Pattani: adit-pachchuban*. (Pattani: Past-Present). Chomromseathean: Bangkok.

Baka, Dolmanach. *Raingan karnvichai ruang karnsob khaosuksa tho khong nakrian Thai Muslim chakrongrianrat songsassan Islam ti mahavityalai Songkla Nakarin doi rabthrong pi karnsuksa 2525*. (Research Report on Examination of the Thai Muslim Students from the Islamic Private School at Prince of Songkla University through Direct Admission in the Academic Year 1982). Pattani: Faculty of Humanities and Social Sciences, South Thailand, n.d. (Mimeograph)

Bunsombat, Wirat., Research Team. *Karnsuksa sathanapab leh panha karnhat karnrian karnson nai radab matyomsuksa thonprai khong rongrian ekkachon sonsassan Islam khet karnsuksasong*. (Study of the status and problem of learning-teaching in High Secondary level of Islamic private schools, Educational Region Two). Pattani: Faculty of Education, Prince of Songkla University, Pattani, South Thailand, 1983. (Mimeograph)

Burutpat, Khachatphai. 1976. *Thai Muslim*. Bangkok: Praephitya.

Center for coordination of administration of the southern border provinces in Yala. *Krongkarn prathom nithed kharachkarn*. (The orientation project for officials). Orientation Division, Personnel Development Unit, Yala, South Thailand, n.d.

Chaipranee, Smarn., Suwanthat, Podo. 1981. *Sapab panha khong karnpatna rongrianrat sonsassana Islam pak tai*. (Situational problem of the reformation of Islamic private school in southern Thailand). Office of Private Education Committee, (Mimeograph)

Educational Region Two. 1983. *Raingan kan prachom suksathikan changwat, suksathikarn amphoe, leh phuchuay suksathikarn amphoe nai khet suksasong*. (Report on the Meeting of Provincial education inspectors, District education inspectors and assistants of District education inspectors in the Educational Region Two). Yala: South Thailand. (Mimeograph)

Kaewdaeng, Rung. 1968. *Thassana khati khong tok kru tokarn prabprong ponok pen rongrianrat sonsassana Islam.* (The Attitude of Religious Teachers towards Reformation of the *Pondok* into the Islamic Private School). M.A. thesis, Sataban Bandeth Pattana Borihansat (NIDA) (The National Institute of Development Administration), Bangkok: Thailand.

Khunthongphet, Chalermkiat. 1986. *Karn totan nayobai rattaban nai si changwat pak tai khong pradeth Thai doi karnnam khong Haji Sulong Abdulkadir.* (The Resistance Against The Government's Policy In The Four southern Provinces of Thailand under Haji Sulong Abdulkadir's Leadership). M.A. thesis, Department of History, Graduate School, Silpakorn University, Bangkok.

Matichon (Bangkok). 10 October 1988.

Matyusof, Berahim. 1985. *Karnboriharn nganvichakarntham krongkan sohnsassana Islam nai rongrian prathomsuksa changwat chaiden pak tai.* (The Academic Administration of the Islamic Studies Teaching Project in Elementary Schools in Southern Bordor Provinces). M.A. thesis, Department of Educational Adminis- tration, Gradaute School, Chulalongkorn University, Bangkok.

Ministry of Education. 1982. *Laksud Islam suksa tonton, tonklang, tonprai pi 2523.* (The curricula of Islamic studies in primary middle, secondary of the year 1980). Bangkok: Aronkarnphim.

Ministry of Education. 1980. *Penkarnson Islam suksa chanprathom suksa pi ti 3-4.* (Teaching plan of Islamic studies for primary levels 3-4). Bangkok: Department of Academy.

Office of Private Education Committee. *Raingan karn patibatngan leh satiti karnsuksa khong rongrianrat sonsassana Islam nai khetsuksasong pi karnsuksa 2524.* (Report on the results of operations and educational statistics of the Islamic private schools in Educational Region Two, Fiscal Year 1981). Yala, South Thailand, 1981. (Mimeograph)

Office of Private Education Committee. *Raingan phonkarnpatibatngan leh satiti kansuksa khong rongrianrat sonsassana Islam nai khetsuksasong pi karnsuksa 2527.* (Report on the results of operations and educational statistics of the Islamic private schools in Educational Region Two, Fiscal Year 1984). Yala, South Thailand, 1984 (Mimeograph)

Office of Private Education Committee. *Raingan phonkarnpatibatngan leh satiti kansuksa khong rongrianrat sonsassana Islam nai khetsuksasong pi karnsuksa 2528.* (Report on the Results of operations and educational statistics of the Islamic private schools in Educational Region Two, Fiscal Year 1985). Yala, South Thailand, 1985. (Mimeograph)

Office of Private Education Committee. *Satiti raichu rongrian ekkachon pised thi pen nayobai pi karnsuksa 2525.* (Statistics of the names of special private schools under the policy of academic year 1982). Bangkok, Ministry of Education, 1982. (Mimeographed.)

Office Board of National Elementary Education with the Cooperation of the Office of Educational Region Two, Yala. *Ekkasan prakob kan summana phu borihan karnsonsassana Islam nai rongrian prathomsuksa changwat chaiden pak tai 2524.* (Paper forwarded in the seminar for administrators of Islamic Teaching in the primary education of the southern border provinces). Yala, south Thailand: Educational Region Two, 1981. (Mimeograph)

Office of Private Education Committee. *Ekkasan prakob karn pramoenphul pattana rongrianrat sonsassana Islam paktai* 2524. (Document prepared for the assessment of the development of Islamic Private Schools in southern Thailand). Yala: Division of special education, south Thailand 1981. (Mimeograph)

Office of Regional Education Inspector, Educational Region Two. *Khumu kru tham krongkarn sonsassana Islam nai rongrian prathomsuksa changwat chaiden pak tai.* (A Teacher's Handbook on the Islamic teaching project at Elementary Schools in southern border provinces). Yala: Division of Teaching Islam in Elementary School, South Thailand, n.d.

Office of Regional Education Inspector, Educational Region Two. *Ekkasan karnvichai phonkarn damnoen tham krongkan sohnsassana Islam nai rongrian prathomsuksa changwat chaiden pak tai.* (Research document on the outcome process of Islamic teaching project in the Primary Schools of southern borders). Yala: Division of Islamic Teaching Project in elementary schools, n.d.

Panchapong, Chaiwat., and Tiansong, Narong. 1975. *Chaettanakati khong prachachon thi mi tosapab kansuksa nai changwat Pattani, Yala leh Narathiwat* 2518. (A Research report on attitudes of the people towards the education in the provinces of Pattani, Yala and Narathiwat). Bangkok: Faculty of Social Sciences and Humanities, Mahidol University.

Prachatippatai (Bangkok). 29 June 1974.

Prince of Songkla University. 1983. *Raingan kan prachom summana phua chattangsûn Islam suksa* 2526. (Seminar Report on the Establishing of Islamic Studies Center). Pattani: South Thailand, Rusamelae Campus.

Prince of Songkla University. *Krongkarn chatthang sathaban Islam suksa.* (The Project of Establishment of Islamic Studies Institute). Pattani: Rusamelae Campus, n.d. (Mimeograph)

Prince of Songkla University. 1986. *Laksod silpasasbandith sakha vicha phasa Arab* 2529. (Curriculum for Bachelor of Arts in Arabic). Pattani: Faculty of Humanities and Social Sciences, Pattani Campus, .

Prince of Songkla University. 1986. *Raingan karnsummana thang vichakarn rueng Islam: withi kan damnuen chiwit* 2529. (Seminar report on Islam: the Way of Life). Pattani: The Establishing Project of Islamic Studies Institute.

Pusawang, Nanthawan. 1978. *Panha chao Thai-Muslim nai si changwat pak tai.* (Problems of Thai-Muslims in the four southern provinces). Bangkok: Social Science Association of Thailand.

Sawanakunanon, Chamlong. 1975. "Botbat khong tok kru rongrianrat sonsassana Islam nai changwat chiden pak tai." (Role of religious teachers of Islamic Private Schools in southern border provinces). M.A. thesis, Faculty of Education, Srinakarinvirot University, Bangkok.

Siamrat (Bangkok). 8 June 1983.

Sutthasat, Arong, Dr. *Panha kuam khatyaeng nai si changwat paktai* 2519. (Problem of Conflict in the Four Southern Provinces). Bangkok: Borisat Phitakpracha Press.

Interviews

'Abd al-Raḥmân Arshadi, Muḥammad bin Ḥaji (1939-1987), Tok Guru Pondok Dalo (Maʻhad al-ʻUlûm al-Sharîfah al-Dalowîyah), Pattani. Interview by writer, 15th September 1986.

'Abd al-Raḥmân 'Abd Allâh bin Ḥaji, Tok Guru's assistant of Pondok Perigi, Yarang, Pattani. Interview by writer, 11th September 1987.

'Abd al-Raḥmân, 'Abd Allah, Ḥaji, Tok Guru's assistant of Pondok Tok Jong, Nongchik, Pattani. Interview by writer, 25th September 1986.

Adam bin, 'Abd al-Raḥmân, Haji, Tok Guru Pondok Bermin (*Madrasah Nur al-Islam al-Berminiyah*), Bermin, Pattani. Interview by writer, 12th September 1986.

Aḥmad Haramayn, Tok Guru's assistant of Pondok Tok Jong, Nongchik, Pattani. Interview by writer, 5th september 1987.

Aḥmad Perigi, Ramlî bin, (Ustâdh), Pondok Perigi (*Madrasah al-Maṣlaḥah al-Islamîyah*), Yarang, Pattani. Interview by writer, 11th September1987.

Aḥmad Perigi, Yaḥya bin, (Tok guru's assistant) Pondok Perigi, Yarang, Pattani. Interview by writer, 11 September 1987.

'Alî Bâkum, Tok Guru Ḥaji Idrîs (Tok Guru Baba Yeh) of Pondok Tok Jong (*Sakulsat Vittaya*), Nongchik, Pattani. Interview by writer, 25 September 1986.

Cerok Keriang Awang, Ḥaji, Tok Guru Pondok Cerok Keriang, (*Bamrong Muslimin*), *Bacok* Saiburi, Pattani. Interview by writer, 2nd September 1987.

Charong, Acharn Manit. (Acharn: a Thai word denotes an intellectual in Thai education), Head of Islamic studies program in government primary schools, Educational Region Two, Yala, Thailand. Interview by writer, 5th Seprtember 1987.

Che' Arong, 'Abd al-Raḥman, Ḥaji (Ustâdh), *Sasnupatam School,* Bana, Pattani. Interview by writer, 22th August 1986.

Chemalee, 'Abd al-Rashîd, Ḥaji, (died November 8th, 1986), Tok Guru Pondok Kok Mee (*al-Muʼassasah al-Khâyrîyah lil-Nahḍah al-Dînîyah*), Hat Yai, Songkhla, Tahiland. Interview by writer, 29th August 1986.

Dâwûd, Qâsem, Ḥaji, Tok Guru's assistant of Pondok Tok Jong (*Sakulsat Vittaya*) *Nongchik*, Pattani. Interview by writer, 26th September 1987.

Habaya, Aḥmad, (Acharn), Office of Educational Region Two, Yala, Thailand. Interview by writer, 5th September 1987.

Ḥâriz Aslam, (The owner of printing house) Ḥariz Trading Book Store, Pattani. Interview by writer, 27th August 1986.

Krabi, Isḥâq, Tok Guru's assistant of Pondok Tok Jong, Nongchik, Pattani. Interview by writer, 5th September 1987.

Luṭfî, Ismaʻil, Dr. (Ustâdh), Pondok Pujud (Bamrong Islam School), Pujud, Pattani. Interview by writer, 31st Audust 1987.

Muhammad Nûr bin, 'Abd al-Laṭîf, Ḥaji, Tok Guru Pondok Jerang batu (*Triam Suksa Vittaya*), Pattani. Interview by writer, 18 September 1986, 2 September 1987.

Mamah, Arom (Acharn), Head of Arabic religious curricular in Islamic private school, Educational Region Two, Yala, Thailand. Interview by writer, 5th september 1987.

Nahdi, Muḥammad, (The owner of printing house), Nahdi Book Store, Pattani. Interview by writer, 27th August 1986 and 14th september 1987.

Raden Aḥmad, Nik 'Arif (Acharn), Educational Region Two, Yala, Thailand. Interview by writer, 5th September 1987.

Sâlim Halabî, Khâlid, (The owner of printing house), Pattani. Interview by Somchet Naksewee and Roheem Niyomdecha, 14th September 1987.

Staff and personnel of Office of Educational Regional Two, Yala, Thailand. Interview by writer, 13th September 1986.

Wan Lembut, Ahmad, (Ustâdh), Director (Mudîr) of *Ma'had Dâr al-Ma'ârif*, Muang, Pattani. Interview by writer, 16th September 1986 and 13th September 1987.

Waba, Nik Mukhtar, Director (Mudîr) of *Darunsat Vitya Islamic High School* (Markaz *al-Dirâsât al-Islâmîyah al-'Aliyah*), Saiburi, Pattani. Interview by writer, 26th September 1987.

Index

'Abd al-Khâliq al-Qudsi, Dr.   122
academic significance   110
adhān   59
administrators   110
Acharn Manich Charong   92, 93
Acharn Pann Yuanlaie   119
Ahmad Samadi   71
ahli al-sunnah wa-al jama'ah 26, 30-31
al-Khulafa' al-Rahshidun   31
Allahu akbar   25
amulets   29
Arkan al-Islam   61
Arābic-religious education   96

baba   34
balaisah   41, 56, 58-59
Ban Plee   65
barakah   36
berkat   56
bid'ah   30
British protection   38
Buddhist doctrine   74
bumi Melayu   29

Cabinet   120
Center Coordination of
      Administration 102, 117, 120
Chaeng Sukhkua, Dr   96
Chana (district)   56
Chartchai Chonhawan, 120
colonizing nations   42
Combodia   28, 38, 44
Creating National Consciousness   74

doa   29
Dutch   42

educational reform policy   74
Educational Region Two   88, 92, 96

Faculty of Humanities and Social
      Sciences   103

fard 'ayn   56, 58
fard kifayah   57
fatwa   23
Fazlur Rahman   66
financial aid   78
financial inducement   78
five southern border provinces   55
fiqh   23

General Education Center   91
General Thai Education   100

hadith   32
hadramawt   23
Haji 'Abd Rashid Radin Ahmad
      Jambu   52
Haji Ahmad Husayn   64
Haji Idris bin Haji Ali Bakum   64
Haji Hamzah 65
Haji Qasem bin Haji Dawud 64
Hālaqat 35
Hashim Non-Añant 119
Herbal pratices 29
Herbs 29
Higher Educational Development
      Plan 110
Hijrah 23
Haris Trading 52
Holy city 39

Ibn Khaldun   57
Ijazah   57, 65
Imam   25, 37, 41
iman   32
important texts   96, 100
Indonesian Societies   42
initial resistance   74
Islamic
      Development Bank(IDB)   119
      education   56, 58
      heritage   69
      precepts   56
      private schools   88

Islamic Secretariat, 119
Isra' and *Mi'*raj 26

Jawi-Arabic intellectual learning 35

kalimah shahadah 47
karamah 28
kedai kitab 22
ketua mutal'ah 62
kitab 22
    Jawi 39, 44, 46, 49, 62
    kuning 52, 54
krabi 57
langgar 55
language instruction programs 88
Latin 42
local Muslim leaders 88
liberal education 103

Malay-Indonesian scene 43
Malay Muslim communities 41-42, 56-
    58, 88
    children 75
    World 36
Malay language 47, 73
Malay peninsular 42
Malay speaking community 50, 61
Malay 29, 43-44
ma'thur 29
madrasah 41, 52, 55, 58, 92
madhhab 24, 26, 30, 50
masa'il 31
Masjid al-Haram 23, 33-36
Masjid al-Nabawi 57
Masjid al-Azhar 57
Masjid Khan 58
matn (the text) 35
Melaka 11, 36-42
middle eastern countries 97-99
Ministry of University
    Affairs 103, 110, 123
Ministry of Education 96-97
Ministry of Foreign Affairs 120
Ministry of Interior 103, 102
modern trend 68
Mohsin 'Abd al-Rahman Abu Si'da,

Prof. 119
mother and mentor 64
mubtada' (*bermula*) 64
Muhammad Abdul Kadir (Dr.) 74
Muhammad Idris Afghan 52
Muhammad Nahdi 52
Muhammad Tawfiq 'Uwaida, Mr. 119
Muslim Philipines 55
Muslim education 73

Nakornsri Thammaraj (Province) 57
Narathiwat (Province) 55
Nathawee (district of Songkla
    Province) 65
National Economic and Social
    Development Plan 117
National Security Council 99, 117, 120
national policy 78
naturalistic etiologies,
    (ta'lil al-mara<u>d</u>) 46

Padang Langga 22
Pangnga (Province) 57
Patthalung (Province) 57
Patani (Province) 22, 28, 31, 35,
    37-40, 46-49, 56
    Malay dialect 28
    scholars 33
penalitas 55
physico-medical treatments 29
Phuket (Province) 57
Pisut Hajidin, a Chargé d'affairs 69
Pondok
    Bermin 53
    Dalo 53
    founders 88
    Haji 'Abd al-'Aziz Naprado 53
    Hutan Agu 65
    Padang Langa 22, 56
    pesantren 55
    Semla 53
pondok dalae and *pondok luar* 59
pondok nai and *pondok nok* 59
Portuguese 42
printing press 39
Promised Day 24
President Gamal Abdel Nasser 69
President Muhammad Anwar Sadat 69

Putra Sultan Muhammad   28

Qouta *Phised*   102
Quran   59
Quranic school (kuttab)   57

Regional Islamic Da 'wah Council of
  Southeast Asia and Pacific
  (Riseap)   120
religous educational system   56
religious leaders   56
rung Kaewdaeng   92

solat   25
solat al-Fajr   59
salawat   29
Satun (Province)   55
Sawat Sakulthai, Dr.   119
secularists   68
Shaykh Hasan al-Tohamy 119
Shaykh Muhammad Abduh   55
Shaykh Yusuf al-Hajji   119
Siamese control   38
Seddik Taouti, Mr.   119, 121
Songkla (Province)   55, 65
Southern Thailand   55
Southeast Asia   55
sufi   24, 28
Supreme Council for Islamic
  Affairs in Cairo   119
surau   56
Suwit Suthanukul, Secretary-General to
  the National Council   120

Takbirat al-Ihram   25
tadika school   65
talisman   29, 46
tariqah   28
tasawwuf   28
Thai and Malay-speaking   56, 59

Thai authority   75
Thai Compulsory Public Education   58
Thai curriculum   100
Thai Education   73, 74, 76
Thai identity   73
Thai Nationalism   74
Thai Students' Association in Cairo 69,
  71
Thai speaking group   41, 50
Thai education   103
tok guru or local ulama   57, 62, 66
Tok Guru Haji Ahmad Perigi   64
Tok Guru Dalo   64
To'khru   57, 59
Tok Qadi   104
Tok Nahu   56
Tok Faqih   56
traditional religious teachers   56
Trang (Province)   57
Tuanku Abdul Rahman   120
Turkish Authortiy   38, 42

ulama   37-41, 44, 50
U.S. based Asia Foundation   119
ustadh   57
Ustaz Ramli   64
Ustazah Hasnah   64
Vichid Srisaan, Mr.   113

wali   28
Wan Kadir Che Man   66
waqf   66
World Assembly of Muslim Youth 121
wudu'   59

Yahya (Haji Ahmad Perigi's son)   64
Yala   55

zakat   66